Endorsements

"Mother Teresa's words to Donna-Marie seem like words to us all. Rather than feeling like we are on the outside looking in, the warmth of the friendship between these two women wraps us all in wisdom, holiness, and love. Most of all, Mother Teresa's messages to Donna encourage us to desire the holiness which she stated is not a luxury for a few but rather everyone's duty."

Patti Maguire Armstrong, Catholic speaker and author
www.raisingcatholickids.com

"Donna-Marie has composed a loving distillation of Blessed Teresa's thought based upon a decade of correspondence and visits with the saint of the ghettos. It is a Tale of Two Mothers, of how a chance meeting of the small, dynamic Albanian nun with a young American housewife became a conduit of grace for many. One comes away convinced that the greatest power under heaven is not wealth or political influence but the loving spirit of a mother, for spiritual motherhood is especially efficacious in bringing a healing touch into the many and intangible Calcuttas of the modern world."

Elena Maria Vidal, author of Trianon
http://teaattrianon.blogspot.com

"Part biography of Blessed Teresa, part memoir of a friendship, *Mother Teresa and Me* offers encouragement, nourishment, and inspiration to people in all walks of life as we encounter, in Blessed Teresa's words, "Calcutta all over the world." Drawing on the life and faith of Blessed Teresa, as well as on a personal friendship with her, Donna-Marie Cooper O'Boyle shares miracles large and small. She paints a picture of a world in which each of us — however distant the goal may seem — can become a saint."

Karen Edmisten, author and blogger
http://karenedmisten.blogspot.com

"Here, at last, is a look at Mother Teresa, not as she stood in the midst of her amazing life, but as she influenced someone we all could know, someone who could live right down the street from you or me. Donna-Marie captures the impact of a friendship few of us can fathom and makes it seem normal, achievable, and in accomplishing that, she makes sainthood not only a nice theory but a goal we want to pursue. In this treasury, we have two women's hearts touching, across miles and vocations, and in the glimpse of their friendship, we see a part of ourselves, and we are inspired."

Sarah Reinhard, http://snoringscholar.blogspot.com

"Through careful discernment, Donna-Marie has kept the story of her friendship with Mother Teresa close to her heart for the last several decades. By sharing it with us now, Donna offers us a gift that she and this modern-day saint began creating years ago — a gift that gently but urgently challenges us to give back by recognizing the streets of Calcutta in our own backyards. Oh, that we might take up this challenge and thereby change the world!"

Roxane Beauclair Salonen, award-winning children's author,
http://roxanesalonen.blogspot.com

MOTHER TERESA
and ME

MOTHER TERESA
and ME

Ten Years of Friendship

DONNA-MARIE COOPER O'BOYLE

Our Sunday Visitor Publishing Division
Our Sunday Visitor, Inc.
Huntington, Indiana 46750

ISBN 978-1-61278-500-4 (Inventory T1204)
LCCN: 2011932120

Cover photo: W.P. Wittman Limited.
Cover design: Tyler Ottinger
Interior design: Sherry Hoffman

PRINTED IN THE UNITED STATES OF AMERICA

Dedication

To my children:

Justin, Chaldea, Jessica,
Joseph, and Mary-Catherine

I love you!

I pray that Mother Teresa's blessings and prayers
for all of you will bear many fruits in your lives!

I also lovingly dedicate this book to dear Blessed
Mother Teresa of Calcutta and to the poor she
loved so unreservedly.

Apostolic Blessing from
Pope John Paul II

Shortly after the beatification of Blessed Teresa of Calcutta in October 2003, Pope John Paul II bestowed his
apostolic blessing "as a pledge of joy and peace in our
Lord Jesus Christ" on Donna-Marie Cooper O'Boyle, her
family, and her "work on Mother Teresa of Calcutta."

TABLE OF CONTENTS

FOREWORD

There are no coincidences in life. Nothing happens by chance, although it may sometimes seem that way. As we read in Scripture, "Every hair on our head is counted" and "His eye is on the sparrow." So it is with all of our lives, which are made up of what I have heard referred to as "Godcidences" verses coincidences. The Lord places us right where we need to be at exactly the right moment.

And so it happened with my dear friend Donna-Marie Cooper O'Boyle and her "chance" meeting after attending a Mass with Blessed Mother Teresa of Calcutta. And so it happened with my "chance" meeting with Donna. It happened online one day as she dropped me an email after listening to my daily radio program. She shared some information about her Website and books. As a syndicated talk-show host I receive hundreds of emails daily, but there was something about Donna's writing, her sincere tone, that led me not only to write back quickly but to almost instantly invite her on my radio program. She has been a regular guest on *Catholic Connection* now with her *Mom's Corner* segment for nearly four years.

As you will see in Donna-Marie's latest work, she was not only deeply moved but profoundly changed by her meeting and subsequent friendship with Mother Teresa. I too have been deeply moved, profoundly changed, and richly blessed by my continuing friendship with an amazing author, speaker, and — most importantly — this sister in Christ.

That's why I was honored when Donna-Marie asked me to write the foreword for this book. Through these pages you will not only get to know Mother Teresa and the late Father John Hardon, a holy and brilliant theologian, but you will also get to know Donna-Marie Cooper O'Boyle, and you will be the better for it.

Donna-Marie's written voice is much like her speaking voice: peaceful, gentle, and lovingly filled with the grace of the Holy Spirit. There is something about her that soothes the soul and calms the nerves. And isn't that just what we need in our hectic lives and our noisy media-saturated culture? I believe these attributes come from Donna-Marie's love of Christ and her devotion to Our Lady and the teachings of the Catholic Church, which were strengthened through knowing Mother Teresa and Father John Hardon and receiving continued support and spiritual advice from both of them. You may also get to know yourself a little better as well, and you may even see yourself among the pages as Donna-Marie walks us through her life with the blessings and challenges of being a mom, a prominent Catholic presenter, and a best-selling writer. Donna introduces you to everyday saints, folks she meets at book signings or conferences who share their love of faith with her and also have a story to tell. You just might be among them.

I was excited to read and learn more about Donna-Marie's friendship with Blessed Mother Teresa because I had an encounter with this Nobel Peace Prize winner myself many years ago. In the summer of 1979 I was a news intern at WJR Radio in Detroit. It was my job to be the hostess, or escort, to the daily guests on one of the Motor City's most popular talk shows at the time, *Focus with J.P. McCarthy*. I was a nominal Catholic in college, but even then I knew that I was encountering great holiness when the tiny woman stepped off the elevator. I brought Mother Teresa into the studio, gave her a glass of water, and then marveled at how she was able to turn the tables on the interviewer. Even as experienced a host as McCarthy was no match for this holy dynamo. Once she found out he was Catholic, she spent most of the thirty-minute interview asking the questions, grilling him about his faith life.

As I escorted her back down to the lobby of the building, we chatted about our namesake, the great mystic and first female doctor of the Church, St. Teresa of Avila, and then Mother Teresa blessed me. Mother Teresa blessed me! I will never forget that day or that moment. Looking back now I realize that this was one of those "Godcidences." Jesus tells us that he will never leave us or forsake us. I have had many struggles in my life, most of which had to do with turning my back on God and the Church for many years. But there were profound moments where God was making his presence known to me. This was definitely one of those times.

In getting to know Donna-Marie over the past few years, I have been offered glimpses into her friendship with Blessed Mother Teresa of Calcutta. But now you and I can hear, as Paul Harvey used to say, "the rest of the story." I don't want to tell you too much about the rest of the story. I want you to experience that for yourself.

It is no coincidence that Donna-Marie met and developed a friendship with Blessed Mother Teresa of Calcutta. It is no coincidence that Donna-Marie and I are now the best of friends. Too many profound events have occurred in our lives as a result of our friendship that we just know the relationship was divinely ordained and a "Godcidence." And it is no coincidence that you are reading this book. Enjoy.

— TERESA TOMEO

INTRODUCTION

In these pages I share my personal encounter and friendship with a humble woman who, by God's grace, transformed countless hearts all over the world. My hope is that this testimony will speak to your heart. I believe the blessings bestowed upon me through the holiness of Mother Teresa must be shared with those who did not have the good fortune to know her personally.

While this book focuses on the life and spirit of Blessed Teresa of Calcutta, it also speaks of other saints in our midst — inspiring people I have met along the way throughout my spiritual journey.

Which raises a few questions.

Who is likely to become a saint? Who would be an unlikely saint? Do extreme piety and obvious holiness always mark sainthood? Does a saint perform his or her duties perfectly, a polished halo hovering overhead? Or can saints be ordinary pilgrims like you and me, following the will of God as we journey toward heaven?

The Catechism of the Catholic Church tells us that "The Church is a 'communion of saints'" (CCC, 960). Yet, typically, our impression of sainthood is that it is reserved for those in heaven and surely must be unobtainable by the likes of you and me.

Perhaps some more than others have the right stuff to become a saint. Others may lead holy and virtuous lives but seem to lack a certain something that, in our minds, should set them apart if we are going to permanently affix the title of "Saint" before their name.

Mother Teresa did not appear remarkable or saintly to her fellow sisters early on. In fact, her small physical stature, combined with her ordinariness, might have suggested a candidate for "Nobody" status.

Yes, she was holy and prayerful. But she appeared unexceptional and seemed frail. She went about her daily routines dutifully and unobtrusively, living out her religious vows without fanfare.

And yet, like all contemplatives, she had a rich interior life. "Holiness is not the luxury of a few," she would eventually begin teaching. "It is everyone's duty: yours and mine."

Above all else, it seemed, Mother Teresa wanted us to know that we are all called to be saints. It is up to us to decide what we will do with that calling.

So it is that saints are in our midst, sometimes hidden from our sight. Other times, the sanctified rub elbows with us sinners in the workplace or marketplace — unobtrusively bringing out the best in us just by showing up.

Mother Teresa explained that St. Thomas Aquinas described holiness as "nothing else but a resolution made, the heroic act of a soul that surrenders to God."

Aren't we fortunate that Mother Teresa let us in on her simple secret to sanctity?

"Holiness does not consist in doing extraordinary things," she would say. "It consists in accepting with a smile what Jesus sends us. It consists in accepting and following the will of God."

Pope Blessed John Paul II told us, "The saints have always been the source and origin of renewal in the most difficult moments in the Church's history... holiness is the hidden source and infallible measure of her apostolic activity and missionary zeal" (CCC, 828). This successor of St. Peter himself will no doubt be canonized a saint one day, if not officially titled John Paul the Great. He happened to have an endearing and holy affection for Mother Teresa. This era of Church history was privileged to receive the benefits of both of these remarkable people.

We also learn from Pope Paul VI, who proclaimed, "We believe in the communion of all the faithful of Christ, those who are pilgrims on earth, the dead who are being purified, and the blessed in Heaven, all together forming one Church; and we believe that in this communion, the merciful love of God and his saints is always [attentive] to our prayers" (CCC, 962).

Mother Teresa said, "The saints are all the people who live according to the law God has given us." Mother Teresa taught us that "the decision to be holy is a very dear one." As you immerse yourself in the pages of this book, perhaps you may sense a prompting in your own soul.

This decision to become holy originates in our hearts and is followed through with our wills. We have to *want* holiness. We had better be aware, though, that the journey to sainthood doesn't imply that we will be carried by angels down a lane adorned with aromatic and beautiful roses, while angelic hymns caress our ears and heavenly consolation fills our senses. Blessed Teresa reminded us that together with the blessings that come to a soul who opts for holiness come also "renunciation, temptations, struggles, persecutions, and all kinds of sacrifices." God's grace will sustain us.

St. Thérèse of Lisieux, a favorite saint of Mother Teresa's, once remarked that she was certainly not "swimming in consolations." Her life was not all bliss and comfort. Yet she embraced it all, wanting to give her whole life — every ounce and every breath, joy, and pain — to her Lord. "My God, I choose everything," she prayed. "I will not be a saint by halves. I am not afraid of suffering for Thee."

God calls us to go forward without hesitation, seeking holiness with hopeful and joyful hearts. If we'll take this small step toward him each day, we can be assured that our labors will not be in vain; rather, they will open the gates of heaven for us — and for all those with whom we have shared our testimonies of his grace by our word and example.

And so I share my testimony of his grace, inspired for this particular project by these words of my friend Blessed Teresa of Calcutta:

We must not attempt to control God's actions. We must not count the stages in the journey he would have us make. We cannot long for a clear perception of our progress along the route, nor long to know precisely where we are on the path of holiness. I ask Jesus to make me a saint. I leave it to him to choose the means that can lead me in that direction. Lord, make me a saint according to your own heart, meek and humble.

Note from the author: The quotes from Mother Teresa that I have used throughout this book are from personal conversations I have had with her and from notes I have taken over the years after hearing her talk to the sisters or during her speeches that I have attended. Some quotes are also from personal letters she sent me, not all of which have been included in this book.

+LDM

Missionaries of Charity,
54A, Lower Circular Rd.
Calcutta 16.

5th October, 1987.

Dear Mrs. Donna,

Thank you very much for your letter
and the beautiful thoughts you have
expressed.

Please continue praying and offering
your sufferings for our Mother - She
needs it most now.

God loves you much and will reward your
generous desire in giving yourself to
His poor.   Keep the joy of loving
through sharing.

God bless you
Teresa mc

One

Surprised by Sanctity

Never in my wildest dreams could I have anticipated an encounter with a recipient of the Nobel Peace Prize, much less a living saint. Yet that's exactly what I experienced one summer morning two decades ago while on a trip to Washington, DC, from my family's home in Connecticut.

Most surprising of all, the "chance" meeting would turn out to be only the beginning of a long and life-changing friendship.

It all started when I sought out Father John Hardon, SJ, the late, great Jesuit theology professor, for spiritual guidance. After helping me for some time over the phone and through written correspondence, he invited my husband, children, and me to Georgetown University for a face-to-face visit.

At some point during our stay, he encouraged us to visit the terminally ill at the Gift of Peace House, part of the nearby Missionaries of Charity convent. I welcomed the opportunity, because I liked to bring my children to nursing homes and hospitals to visit the sick and lonely. The side trip would prove to be a profound and indescribable experience.

After observing the sisters care for the dying with smiles, tenderness, and compassion, I began to understand why the patients seemed so at peace despite their suffering: They were immersed in genuinely selfless love.

Later I would learn that Mother Teresa and the sisters taught the patients about redemptive suffering, encouraging them not to "waste" their pain and explaining that God could sanctify it if they offered it to him through prayer.

We felt honored when the sisters invited us to return the next day for Mass in their chapel. When they told us Mother Teresa would be at one of the Masses, we were awestruck. We had no idea she was even in the United States, much less so close to where we were staying.

There was some talk about us possibly meeting Mother Teresa, but all I could think to say was that I wouldn't want to take up her time. After all, I thought, this is a woman who has brought peace among peoples and solace to the poor all over the world. Who were we to keep her from her wondrous work?

That's not to say that I wasn't excited about our prospects for a brush with greatness. On the contrary — I said a quick prayer to put the whole thing in God's hands.

For no particular reason, we decided on the early Mass. This would mean rousing the kids at five in the morning to allow time for the ride from our hotel.

Upon arriving at the convent, we noticed many pairs of sandals lined up outside the chapel door. We slipped off our shoes and placed them at one end. Then we entered, filing in as quietly as possible for a family with three small children. A quick glance around the interior revealed its austerity. There were no pews, chairs, or kneelers. We knelt among the nuns on the bare chapel floor.

It was apparent the sisters took care of this little chapel not out of dry duty but with great love. The room was stark, but not a speck of dust lay on the shiny hardwood floor. Meanwhile the saris of the Missionaries of Charity enveloped us in a miniature sea of white and blue. The sisters knelt, heads bowed, praying quietly. My family tried to settle in without being too conspicuous. In reality, I'm sure we stood out like neon signs.

After a short while, as I prayed and kept watch over my children, I noticed a small, hunched figure enter the chapel. "There she is!" I thought. "We came to the right Mass." I told myself to get my attention back on my prayers and on the Mass that was about to begin, not on the fact that there was a living saint in our midst.

Mother Teresa glided past us, her bare feet making feather-light sounds on the floor. Her wrinkled hands were clasped tightly and held close to her heart. I could sense an awesome presence as she passed by. I momentarily lifted my eyes to take a little more in. Her height — or lack thereof — took me by surprise. This spiritual giant stood not much taller than my six-year-old daughter.

I was also struck by the prominence of the hump in her back. This, of course, developed during all those years stooping over to serve the poor, sick, and dying confined to floor mats.

No one made a fuss over Mother Teresa as she knelt down and blended in. While the sisters' hearts must have been silently soaring over the presence of their mother-foundress, it was as though she were just another member of the family taking her place at table.

The priest and his "congregation" celebrated the Mass in a way that made me see fresh beauty in the old but ever-new liturgies of the Word and the Eucharist. The sisters sounded like angels singing the hymns, and the priest's homily pierced my heart.

As for my children, their behavior was angelic, too — up to a point. After a while my youngest, Jessica, started showing signs of restlessness in the small, sweltering chapel. Several times I carried her out of the chapel, hoping to settle her, then tiptoed back inside.

My daughter Jessica gazes into Mother Teresa's eyes — a gaze that lasted quite awhile and caused a hush to come over all who were present.

"A little child will lead them..."

Given my concern about my children disrupting the sisters' Mass, it was ironic that they drew Mother Teresa to me.

When Mass ended, one of the sisters was moved by the sight of my six-year-old, Chaldea, genuflecting before the Blessed Sacrament. My heart warmed as I watched the sister go out of her way to give Chaldea a big hug.

All at once I realized: That's not just any sister — *that's Mother Teresa!*

Then, as quickly as she'd moved into the picture, she moved back out again, exiting the chapel for another room in the convent.

My family left the chapel and stood in the foyer for awhile, taking in the moment and trying to digest the blessings we'd just received. As if it hadn't been enough to share Mass in a chapel filled with Missionaries of Charity and witness the power of their prayer, we'd even gotten a hug from their powerful and world-famous foundress.

"What," we asked aloud, "could ever top this?"

Just then, the door opened from across the foyer, and Mother Teresa came straight toward me and two-year-old Jessica, secure in my arms so she couldn't run around the convent.

Mother Teresa's surprise approach was direct yet gentle.

"Is this the baby who was singing at Mass?" she asked me.

"Yes!" I replied.

It seemed as if everything moved in slow motion as Mother Teresa of Calcutta, dressed in her simple white sari trimmed in Blessed Mother blue, reached out her worn, loving hand to touch my daughter and pat her back.

In fact, I think my heart stopped for that moment. This same woman who traveled the world ministering to the "poorest of the poor," a woman highly regarded by popes and presidents and millions of people, had just spoken to ... *me*. The same hand that comforted God's beloved lepers, that consoled the most desperate of the dying, was reaching out and touching my little Jessica.

Mother Teresa kissed a Miraculous Medal and handed it to Jessica. Then she did the same for my husband, me, Chaldea, and Justin, my son.

Our conversation, after my initial surprise, flowed easily and naturally.

Now, reminiscing all these years later, it seems as though those moments are suspended in time. That first encounter with this saint (as of this writing, she has been beatified, and I have no doubts about her eventual canonization) penetrated my heart and etched an unforgettable message that remains to this day.

I think that, in a certain sense, standing next to Mother Teresa was like standing near Jesus Christ himself. I had the sense of feeling wildly exhilarated and deeply calmed all at once.

We conversed for a while, and then Jessica squirmed to get down from my arms. Mother Teresa stretched out her arms and summoned little Jessica to her side. Without hesitation, my little girl, always timid with strangers, made a beeline for the nun. The two of them held hands, and Jessica looked straight into Mother Teresa's eyes. The room went silent as everyone present watched, amazed at the duration of their gaze.

That was when Mother Teresa told me that Jessica might become a sister of the Missionaries of Charity one day. That wouldn't be the only time that she would tell me this.

As we stood in that intimate and holy setting, Mother Teresa pointed out how fortunate my children were to be part of a family. She said she was accustomed to ministering to abandoned, starving orphans — including babies. I told her how graced I considered myself to be raising children and how blessed I'd been to live out my vocation as a mother.

We talked a while longer before I figured we might be keeping her from her "real" work. We bid our goodbyes, exchanging uninhibited hugs. I recall feeling like I was hugging an old friend, not at all a new one I'd only just met.

Mother Teresa asked our prayers for her and for the poor. She promised her prayers for us. I honestly did not think I would ever meet her face-to-face again. After all, we would soon return to Connecticut, and she'd be off to Calcutta. While I knew I would cherish the blessings of this day as long as I lived, I expected life to go on with its normal schedules and routines, challenges and joys. Those extraordinary moments at the convent would soon enough be fond but fading memories.

How wrong I was about that!

But more on Mother Teresa and me later. First, let's consider who Mother Teresa was to the Church, to the world — and to history.

+LDM

Missionaries of Charity,
54A, Lower Circular Rd.
Calcutta 16.

14th November, 1987.

Dear Donna,

This brings you my prayers and best wishes
and those of my Sisters and the poor.
Continue to bring others to Jesus through
Mary - Be the sunshine of His love and
compassion to them and bring many souls
to God.

God loves you - give Him your heart to
love - Your will to serve Him - pray the
Rosary daily our Blessed Lady will lead
you to her Son. Keep the joy of the
Lord as your strength.

God bless you
Gc Teresa mc

Two

"I Will Be Your Light"

"Love is not words. It is action. Our vocation is to love." That's how Blessed Mother Teresa of Calcutta answered, more than once, when asked to describe the heart of her religious order's mission.

Recalling Blessed Teresa's uncompromising dedication at her beatification in Rome in October 2003, Blessed John Paul II put into words what so many already knew in their hearts. "Her life was a radical living and a bold proclamation of the Gospel," he said. "As a real mother to the poor, she bent down to those suffering various forms of poverty. Her greatness lies in her ability to give without counting the cost, to give 'until it hurts.'"

And yet, great as she became, Mother Teresa was, in many ways, an ordinary woman. Slight, unassuming, outwardly frail, she probably struck many as sickly or delicate of constitution. How did she muster the courage, strength, and grace it surely took to love — really love — the poorest of the poor? From what interior power source did she summon the wherewithal to act on, let alone make sense of, the directions she felt she was receiving from God? And how did her simple message of love come to affect our world so profoundly?

To answer those kinds of questions, let's consider the events that led up to her transformation — which began when she first said "Yes" to God.

Agnes Gonxha Bojaxhiu (pronounced AG-ness GOHN-jay boh-yah-JOO) was born August 26, 1910, and baptized in Skoplje, Albania (on the Balkan peninsula in southeastern Europe). Her Albanian parents, Nikola and Drane, provided a comfortable life for their relatively affluent family. As the youngest of three children, Agnes learned the normal lessons and enjoyed the sweet delights of a childhood without want. Their comforts evaporated in 1919, when the man of the house died.

Fortunately, the children's mother had taught them the habit of prayer. This became a lifeline, helping the family through the crisis of the loss even though it didn't

My son Justin holding the Miraculous Medal just received from Mother Teresa, and my daughter Chaldea receiving a blessing.

fill their hungry stomachs or calm their worried minds — not directly, anyway. The sadness and challenges that followed their beloved father's death strengthened the family's character. They worked hard together to overcome their grief and adjust to life without a powerful breadwinner.

Agnes knew from the time she was twelve years old that Jesus was calling her by name to a different life than most people lived. In fact, as she would later relay, her heart told her she would one day be betrothed to the Lord, cleaving to him unconditionally as a consecrated religious.

Earlier, when she made her first holy Communion at five years old, she'd realized how deeply she cared about the salvation and sanctification of souls — especially the souls of the poor. What she couldn't have understood at so young an age was that God would one day ask her to not only serve the impoverished but also to become one of them.

The Bojaxhiu family belonged to Sacred Heart Church, a Catholic community administered by the Society of Jesus (the Jesuits). Although Agnes remained true to the Catholic faith throughout her childhood, her awareness of God's earlier calling waned as her teen years progressed. That changed when she turned eighteen. Once more her heart awakened to the desire for the consecrated life.

In 1928, with her mother's blessing, Agnes left her home in Skoplje to join the Sisters of Our Lady of Loreto in Ireland. After she'd spent a few months of prayer and contemplation on the Emerald Isle, her superiors sent her to India — first Calcutta and then Darjeeling — to begin her novitiate.

Eight years passed before Agnes professed permanent vows. She chose the name Teresa, after St. Thérèse of Lisieux, using the Spanish spelling because a fellow sister already had the French version. She wanted to model her life not after the "big" Teresa — of Avila, a giant presence in the Church — but after the "little" Thérèse, who was then a very new saint (she was canonized in 1925).

Mother Superior sent Sister Teresa back to Calcutta to live at the Loreto convent and work as a teacher. The young nun taught geography to young girls, mostly of European descent and from affluent backgrounds. Sister Teresa's superiors and peers considered her a gifted teacher. Her students loved her. For her own part, Sister Teresa was content serving as a member of the faculty at clean and peaceful St. Mary's School.

On May 24, 1937, Sister Teresa made her final profession of vows, becoming, as she said, the spouse of Jesus for all eternity. She continued teaching at St. Mary's, and, in 1944, became the school's principal. She would give the school twenty years of devoted, selfless service.

All the while she knew that, outside the confines of the convent, conditions around the city couldn't have provided any sharper a contrast to her little world. Disease ran rampant. Suffering and squalor were everywhere. Noise was inescapable. From time to time, when called to various tasks and duties, she would witness this "other world" firsthand.

The sights, smells, and sounds of the destitute struggling to survive surely tugged on compassionate Sister

Teresa's heart. Yet it wasn't her sensitivity or empathy per se that would later draw her to a life in some of the most wretched places on earth.

A "call within a call"

On September 10, 1946, Sister Teresa boarded a train for her yearly retreat in Darjeeling. During the trip, a remarkable thing happened. She distinctly heard Jesus Christ telling her that her life would be redirected in a wholly unexpected and profoundly new way. She received what she described from that day forward as "a call within a call." She had said yes to God's call to the religious life eighteen years prior, and now she would say yes again. September 10 is still celebrated each year by the Missionaries of Charity sisters as "Inspiration Day."

Sister Teresa became increasingly aware of Jesus' thirst for love and souls. Her heart only desired to satiate her Lord's thirst. During the next few months, she received interior locutions and visions. Jesus exposed the desire of his heart for "victims of love," she later explained, who would "radiate his love on souls." The Lord showed her how he anguished over the world's neglect of the poor. He also expressed his sadness over the world's indifference to him, and he made her know how deeply he hungered for people's love. These intense messages from Jesus continued for quite some time.

As soon as a doubt over the veracity of these messages would enter her mind, Sister Teresa pushed it away. She believed she couldn't be imagining an experience so vivid and so clearly compatible with Scripture and Church teachings. Convinced that the Lord was asking her to leave the comfortable routine of life as a Sister of Loreto, she began to prepare her heart to tread an unfamiliar path caring for the poorest of the poor.

Still, before making a move toward answering her new calling, she knew she had to pray long and hard to discern what specific steps God was pointing her to take.

Sister Teresa had always felt concerned about the poor and unfortunate, praying for them often and earnestly, but she never dreamed that God would ask her to leave her fellow sisters and her students. He was making it clear, however, that she would need to actually become one of the poor in order to fully understand their plight and serve them with a deep, unconditional, and passionate solidarity.

"Come be my light," Our Lord beckoned Sister Teresa, beginning on that train ride. Although she wanted to comply, she wondered for a moment if the Lord should perhaps call someone else — someone more worthy. He wanted her, though, and he wanted her to reach his poor in places where he was unaccepted. She knew this, because he told her.

Bit by bit, Jesus enlightened her about his plan. He wanted missionaries in India who would be Sisters of Charity. They would be his fire of love among the very poor, the stricken, the dying — young and old, alone and in families. The Lord promised her that he would be with her at all times. He assured her that her new life would be intense, difficult, and seemingly impossible at times, but that he would never leave her without sufficient grace to persevere.

She believed even as she trembled inside with natural human trepidation. In fact, years later, this heroic soul would explain that leaving the familiarity of the Loreto convent involved a far more painful sacrifice than she'd endured when she said goodbye to her family years before in pursuit of her initial religious vocation.

But her mind was made up. Her heart was set. She would abandon herself to the Lord with unconditional surrender to his will.

"I," she prayed, "will be your light."

+LDM

Missionaries of Charity
54 A, Lower Circular Road,
Calcutta - 16.

19th January 1988.

Dear Donna,

Thank you very much for your kind letter
and for sharing your inspiration with me.

Thank God for His love for you, for His
presence in you and the joy with which
you want to adore Him in the Blessed
Sacrament by establishing perpetual
adoration of the Blessed Sacrament.

God's ways are wonderful. Its wonderful
to know that you are growing in love with
Jesus the proof that praying together is
the surest way to great holiness.

Keep up the good you are doing and the joy
of loving Jesus in each other and in all
you meet.

God bless you
lee Teresa mc

Three

FAITHFUL STEPS

Exercising due diligence and following normal protocol, the hierarchy of the Catholic Church carefully reviewed Sister Teresa's proposal. During this two-year period, the nun was in correspondence with Calcutta Archbishop Ferdinand Perier, SJ. She shared with him the inner locutions and directives she'd received from Jesus. She explained that the desire to satiate the longings of our Lord increased with every Mass and holy Communion.

Sister Teresa later explained that she received a plan on how to structure the Missionaries of Charity from Jesus during these Masses and during her recollection after receiving Jesus in holy Communion at each Mass.

On August 17, 1948, Sister Teresa donned her new habit, the now-familiar white cotton sari with blue trim (in honor of the Blessed Mother). She left the peaceful order of the Loreto convent for the unpredictable — sometimes dangerous — streets of the poor. No longer a nun in the precise definition of the word — it properly applies only to cloistered women religious, although it's often used informally and affectionately to refer to any consecrated woman in a religious order — she would now be known as Mother Teresa. She went from Sister to

Mother because she was the foundress of a new religious order in the Church.

After being instructed in a short medical course, Mother Teresa entered the slums of Calcutta on December 21, 1948. She began her work with the children, teaching them in an open-air school and drawing lessons in the dirt on the ground. To reward good schoolwork, she handed out pieces of soap: small treasures for children to whom basic cleanliness was a luxury.

To find the children in greatest need, Mother went into parks, dustbins, and other places where parents without hope had disposed of their own flesh and blood. Many of these unwanted little ones were sick with leprosy or other communicable diseases that frightened their families.

The unwanted, the unloved, the uncared for — these Mother Teresa saw as "Jesus in disguise." At first, this must have taken a tremendous act of the will. But, day by day, she put one foot in front of the other, rosary beads in hand. She obeyed. She trusted. She looked past the repulsive and saw only the redeemable. At some point, it became evident that she really did see Jesus in the faces of the poor.

She asked the Lord to send her help and, one by one, helpers arrived. Among the novices were a number of former students she'd taught in the convent schools in Darjeeling and Calcutta. We can only imagine the deep joy she must have felt in those early years, seeing her former students "file in" to learn, take vows, put on the habit of the Missionaries of Charity, and serve Jesus Christ by loving the poor.

The work got the Church's full imprimatur in Calcutta on October 7, 1950. On that day, in the little chapel at 14 Creek Lane, Archbishop Perier established the foundress and her first eleven companions as a Religious Congregation of Diocesan Right.

Choosing humility

By now the name Mother Teresa is synonymous with authentic humility. This is fitting. She never desired fame and, in fact, despised the attention she inadvertently drew. She particularly loathed being treated like a celebrity in the limelight.

At some point, when she realized there would be no escaping the cameras and microphones, Mother Teresa made a deal with God. She asked him to release a soul from purgatory every time someone photographed her. Understanding that God is very creative when it comes to reaching souls, she recognized a chance to spread grace when she saw one.

To humbly serve the poor devotedly and passionately, Mother Teresa armed herself with deep daily prayer. She professed a profound vow of poverty. She became poor herself, vehemently opposed to riches, owning less than the barest of necessities. In this way, she felt she could serve the poor less encumbered, totally focused, and truly understanding of their plight.

Mother Teresa's poverty of spirit was distinctly Franciscan; she loved the way of uncompromising discipleship modeled by Sts. Francis and Clare in the early thirteenth century. She also recognized the rightness of St. Thérèse's insights. "We cannot all do great things," the saint had said, famously, "but we can all do little things with great love." It was Thérèse, of course, whose name she took when she entered the religious life.

From the very beginnings of the Missionaries of Charity, Mother Teresa made a conscious decision to be totally docile before, and dependent upon, God's divine providence. She wanted nothing more than what God chose to give her, the sisters, and the poor. "I fear just one thing," she said. "Money! Greed — the love of money — was what motivated Judas to sell Jesus."

But Mother Teresa also made it clear she did not want social workers. She wanted disciples of Christ. She trained the sisters in prayer as well as action, insisting that they seek Jesus' love for them. Only then, she stressed, would they be able to spread his love to the poor rather than their own, imperfect human love.

"When we come back in the evening, we have one hour of adoration before Jesus in the Blessed Sacrament," she said, "and at this you will be surprised: we have not had to cut down our work for the poor. The one hour of adoration is the greatest gift God could give a community because ... we love the poor with greater and deeper faith and love."

Mother's "extreme" love for the poor

One day, at the very beginning of Mother Teresa's ministry, she came upon a woman lying on a sidewalk. It was clear the woman was dying. Mother Teresa desperately wanted to alleviate the woman's suffering and provide a bed so that she could die peacefully, away from the clamor and squalor of the streets. She managed to get the woman to a hospital, but the medical staff refused to take her in. Mother Teresa would not budge. She insisted on care for the dying woman until, finally, a health worker agreed to help.

This act led to the setting up of the first Home for the Dying and Destitute in Calcutta. The Missionaries of Charity named it *Nirmal Hriday* (which means "Pure Heart"). In time, Mother Teresa went on to open up similar homes and hospices all over the world.

Mother Teresa and the sisters also began to offer the dying a "ticket to heaven" — their clever euphemism for a Christian baptism. They never force the sacrament on anyone, but neither do they neglect to make the offer. Mother Teresa often said that many thousands of dying souls had accepted baptism in the Missionaries' homes. "Of those who have died in our houses, I have never seen anyone die in despair or cursing," she said. "They have all died serenely."

Mother Teresa taught her sisters to "beg the Lord" for an extreme love of the poor. She trained them to begin their day trying to see Jesus through the Eucharist in holy Mass. She explained to them that they are Jesus to others, and they are to seek him in the people they serve.

Throughout each day the Missionaries of Charity connect with Jesus in two profoundly physical ways: first, under the appearance of consecrated bread and wine, and second, under the appearance of the devastated bodies of the poorest of the poor. She tells the sisters to do everything "with Jesus, for Jesus, and toward Jesus" so that their lives become a prayer.

That is certainly what happened to Mother Teresa herself. Looking back on her early days with the Missionaries of Charity, Mother Teresa said that, had she not picked up that first dying woman on the street, she may not have picked up the fifty thousand after. She always said: "Jesus comes to meet us. To welcome him, let us go to meet him."

Jesus comes to meet us in a variety of appearances and disguises. He is hungry, he is naked, he is lonely. He is the alcoholic, the drug addict, the prostitute, and the street beggar. Mother Teresa often admonished, "If we reject them, if we do not go out to meet them, we reject Jesus himself."

This is consistent with the teaching of St. John in the Scriptures. Writing about our duty to love God and our neighbor, he says, "You are a liar if you say that you love God but do not love your neighbor" (1 Jn 4:20). Mother Teresa preached this gospel of love through her caring hands and her tender heart. Seldom did she have occasion, time, or even the desire to preach to masses of people. She did most of her "preaching" by talking to each person she met one-on-one — and, even more, by leading through example. She was drawn to people of every race and creed, reserving special affection for society's sick and outcast, and she liked to get to know each individual on his or her own terms.

Mother Teresa was appalled by the lack of love throughout the world. It deeply saddened her that so many people are unloved even by members of their own families. When she did have occasion to speak to groups of people, she usually used the opportunity to urge defense of the most vulnerable members of the human family: the unborn, the elderly, those in need of constant care and assistance. The very idea of abortion sickened her, nevermind its actual toll on beautiful babies, and she was greatly disturbed by the reality of elderly people left in nursing homes to endure the slow approach of death all alone.

The Gospel of Matthew strengthened and drove Mother Teresa in her resolve to follow God's will in serving the poorest of the poor: "Come, you who are blessed by my Father, inherit the kingdom prepared for you from the foundation of the world; for I was hungry and you gave me food, I was thirsty and you gave me something to drink, I was a stranger and you welcomed me, I was naked and you gave me clothing, I was sick and you took care of me, I was in prison and you visited me" (Mt 25:34–37).

The power of love and the truth of the Gospel, along with Mother Teresa's insatiable desire to quench Jesus' thirst for souls, compelled Mother Teresa to seek out Jesus in everyone with whom she came in contact. She never let an outside appearance of poverty, arrogance, hatred, or any other repellent quality get in the way of seeing through all of it to the Jesus who dwelled within, the Jesus she'd made a promise to love passionately and not count the cost. She referred to the outer appearance of each person as the "distressing disguise."

Blessed John Paul II captured the essence of Mother Teresa of Calcutta with illuminative brevity when he beatified her on October 19, 2003. "In Mother Teresa's smile, words, and deeds," said the Holy Father, "Jesus again walked the streets of the world as the Good Samaritan."

+LDM

Missionaries of Charity,
54A, Lower Circular Rd.
Calcutta 16.

18th February 1988

Dear Donna,

Thank you very much for your letter
and all t e news, two enclosed
photographs and your prayers.

Pray the Rosary daily and ask Our
Blessed Lady to lead you to know
God's will for you. Help our Sisters
in Bronx whenever it is possible.

If we pray, it will be easy for us
to accept suffering. In all our
lives suffering has to come.
Suffering is the sharing in the
Passion of Christ. Suffering is
the kiss of Jesus, a sign that
you have come so close to Jesus
on the Cross that He can kiss you.
Do offer some of your sufferings
for us and our people.

Assuring you of our prayers and
those of our poor.

God bless you

Four

PEN PALS AND MORE

What could possibly top a personal encounter with such holiness as I saw in Mother Teresa that day in Washington, DC? Nothing.

Or so I thought.

We traveled back to the reality of everyday home life in Connecticut. On the trip back, I was feeling much more contemplative than when we set out. The sense of grace at work was almost overwhelming.

I took out pen and paper and began to record a few thoughts. One notion that kept recurring was: "Why not try to communicate further with Mother Teresa?" This desire prodded me throughout the seven-hour ride home.

Again, my initial reaction to the thought was negative. I didn't want to take any time from her vital work. After some serious soul-searching, I decided to call the mother superior of the convent we'd visited. It couldn't hurt to ask her advice on what I should do next.

Mother Superior gave me Mother Teresa's address in Calcutta and encouraged me to write her directly. "Are you sure?" I asked. "Yes, Donna," she answered. Taking this unhesitating affirmation as a bit of divine inspiration, I resolved to follow through with a thank-you note to Mother Teresa.

And so my first letter went out to Mother Teresa in India. It included a simple expression of thanks for the blessings she'd given us by sharing her time and patience. And I told her a bit more about myself.

A few weeks passed. You can imagine my delight when, one otherwise average day, an envelope turned up in my mailbox with a return address in Calcutta. Wow! I literally trembled with anticipation as I opened the envelope. Folded up inside was a typed, single-spaced, one-page letter.

Here I am (pregnant with my son Joseph) with Mother Teresa at one of the Bronx convents.

I carefully unfolded the page and read Mother Teresa's message to me, drinking in each word while my mind flashed back to the unforgettably holy face I'd encountered in the convent weeks before. The words conveyed Mother's gratitude and offered me encouragement and spiritual direction. I recognized the dark black ink and slightly askew lettering as that of an old, manual typewriter. (Do they still make ribbons for those, or was Mother Teresa re-inking an old ribbon over and over again? I never did ask.)

More than her words, it was the realization that Mother Teresa had taken the time to respond to a suburban mom in America that moved me so deeply. The world-renowned caregiver of the poor ended her letter with: "God loves you much and will reward your generous desire in giving yourself to His poor. Keep the joy of loving through sharing. God bless you. M. Teresa MC."

I had no idea that this was only the first of many such correspondences. But, to my continuing amazement even to this day, that's exactly what it was.

Eventually, the letters became familiar visitors to my mailbox, and their tone grew comfortable and natural. I felt like I was simply swapping stories with a dear friend. Still, the letters never failed to give me pause at my mailbox every time I discovered a new envelope with the Calcutta return address.

I recall one occasion when, overcome by emotion to find myself holding yet another letter from Mother Teresa in my hands, I put a hand to my heart and said a prayer to God. My children looked up at me, not sure what to make of my behavior. How relieved they were to find out

Mommy wasn't sad or scared or worried — she was happy with a joy so strong that it almost made her cry.

Intense blessings

As the letters became a regular part of my life, I sensed that the blessings coming to my family through the touch of Mother Teresa were intense and deeper than I could fathom. All I could do was thank God every day. I didn't have time to wonder why these blessings had come to us and not, for example, another family in our neighborhood, town, or state. I was busy raising my family, pushing through the many challenges of modern life and facing some larger trials as well.

I decided to keep my correspondence with this "living saint" on the quiet side. For one thing, I wanted to avoid the temptation to feel pride — especially over something God had put together, not me. I also wasn't sure people would understand. And I certainly did not want to sound like I was bragging.

Twenty-one more letters came from Mother Teresa of Calcutta over the next ten years. Each dispatch brought news, spiritual instruction, a request for prayers, and a promise of prayers from herself and her poor. Mother Teresa typed all the letters on that old typewriter, I learned, usually in the middle of the night after she'd finished with her duties. Every word brought me peace; every message seemed to say just what I needed to hear. This power would prove especially extraordinary when a particularly troubling situation developed in my life.

Over the years, I made countless trips to Missionaries of Charity convents. I got to visit the sisters, listen to retreats led by Father Hardon, and attend profession liturgies for new sisters and brothers. I knew that many graces surrounded these holy people and that there was much for us to learn from them. I was happy that my children would be directly influenced by their holiness, so I brought them whenever I could.

I guess you could say that, at some point, I became something of a Mother Teresa "groupie." That was never my intention, of course, although I am certain that Our Lord put an intense desire in my heart to be near her and to communicate with her about spiritual matters. A couple of times when I visited the sisters in the Bronx, a few of them ended up hopping into my car. With a gleam in their eyes, they would bubble over with joy at the opportunity to see their saintly foundress at whatever nearby convent Mother Teresa was visiting. The sisters loved their Mother and could hardly restrain their enthusiasm for her presence among them.

I would end up seeing Mother Teresa more than a dozen times in the United States. By the grace of God, I was also privileged to gain private audiences with Mother Teresa at her many convents as well. As if that wasn't enough, one day Blessed Teresa and I spoke by long-distance phone — Calcutta to Connecticut — at a time when I desperately needed guidance and prayer.

I can't go into detail about my situation. Suffice it to say that, like most everyone, I went through some personal difficulties through which I could not have made it on my own. God's grace entered through the darkness of my trial. The Lord answered my prayers and sent my blessed mentor to my rescue.

During these moments, I felt privileged beyond description. After all, I was no better or more deserving of Mother Teresa's personal attention than any one of millions of other lay women around the world. Why me? One day I'll ask God that very question.

One observation came through over and over again as I communicated with this living saint at this phase of my life: Mother Teresa was no stranger to real-life struggles. She had seen it all. She knew firsthand about the complications of modern life — just how untidy and even downright nasty it can be. She was not one to shrink from these realities, and she certainly wasn't afraid to engage them head-on.

Back to my urgent, long-distance phone conversation with Mother Teresa. It happened in 1993, and, believe me, it was harder to get a phone connection to Calcutta then than it is now. The phone lines were tricky, and the difference in time zones needed to be considered as well.

An awful lot of prayers and determination went into that phone call that particular day. How amazing was it that the globe-trotting servant of the poor just happened to be at her motherhouse in Calcutta right then, and just happened to answer the phone right there? By the unlikely instant connection alone, I believe, God's hand was at work.

As for her words, they penetrated my heart. I had no doubt that I would be able to survive the major trial God was allowing me to undergo. Mother's wise counsel gave me peace that surpassed all understanding. Nor was she done with that one call. She followed up by writing a letter in which she reiterated what she'd said over the phone and promised more prayers.

She also thanked me for starting a branch of the Lay Missionaries of Charity at my parish. This, I thought, was the least I could do!

My own "call within a call"

I suppose that in a certain sense you could say that, like Mother Teresa, I too received a kind of "call within a call" in my life. This is not to suggest that I saw myself as being in the same league with a woman who, I believe, is certain to become a canonized saint. On the contrary: I believe that, by Mother's example, God beckoned me to answer the Church's universal call to holiness with much greater conviction than I'd ever practiced before.

You see, at the time I met Mother Teresa, I was serving as prioress for a Dominican lay group known as a "third order." I had started this group in my parish along with a friend. The idea was to fill a need for Catholics who wanted to come together to forge a deeper, more personal prayer life.

After meeting Mother Teresa, my heart was transformed. My desire to seek Jesus in the poor increased. I prayed for months and sought spiritual direction. In short, I now believe I was drawn, if not directly pointed, to lay service with the Missionaries of Charity. I understood this new calling to be what God had really wanted of me all along. I also understood it as a continuation, not a refutation, of my calling to the Dominican third order.

After receiving permission from the hierarchy of the Third Order of St. Dominic to leave the group, I became a lay Missionary of Charity. Then, at the request of the sisters, I founded a branch of the lay Missionaries of Charity in my parish.

With that, Mother Teresa wrote me these words: "God will bless you for all the good you have done in starting the lay Missionaries of Charity in New Milford. Be assured of my prayers. Christ calls us to be one with Him in love through unconditional surrender to His plan for us. Let us allow Jesus to use us without consulting us by taking what He gives and giving what He takes."

Now I knew that God had not only transformed my heart. He had changed my very life.

MISSIONARIES OF CHARITY
54A, A. J. C. BOSE ROAD
CALCUTTA-700016

5th October, 1988

Dear Donna,

Thank you very much for your kind letter dated
1st September, 1988.

I am glad to know your desire to become a lay Missionaries of Charity.

Pray to our Lady — pray the Rosary very fervently
cling to Our Lady, She will surely lead you to
Jesus to know His will for you.

Keep the joy of loving Jesus ever burning in your
heart and share this joy with others by your
thoughtful love and humble service.

I assure you of my prayers and those of our poor.

God bless you
M Teresa mc

Five

Hearing God in Harlem

One Friday morning in the spring of 1988, I found myself standing before the door of the Missionaries of Charity convent in Harlem, New York. In one hand I clutched my rosary beads. I used the other hand to knock on the door. After what seemed like an eternity, the enormous door creaked open. I slipped inside the convent, safe from some of New York City's meanest streets.

I had never been to Harlem before, and yet there I was, a mother of three with one on the way (although I didn't know it yet), arriving in the ghetto for a retreat-like experience. The invitation to come here represented a unique opportunity for me, as I was so rarely separated from my family. I would miss them dearly, but this stay was to refresh my spirit and renew my faith — something that would benefit the whole family. I was eager to spend time with the sisters and hear what Our Lord would speak to my heart.

It was Father John Hardon who had invited me here for a weekend of prayer and activities with the sisters. A Jesuit priest widely considered to be one of the best theologians of his time, Father Hardon was also a simple man deeply in love with God. I felt so privileged when, in 1987, he agreed to be my spiritual director. (The cause for his beatification and canonization is under way. For the latest, go to www.hardonsj.org.) By the time I arrived at the Harlem convent, I had been steeped in his guidance through personal visits, letters, retreats, and his books. Quite often Father Hardon would say, while leading a retreat or speaking in conversation, "There's work to be done!" That seemed like a perfect catchphrase for my three-day sojourn in the Harlem convent.

Father Hardon would be giving a retreat to the sisters throughout the weekend. The retreats he gave to laypeople were always filled to capacity, and those who wished to receive his personal attention needed to put their names on long waiting lists. I knew how fortunate I was to reap the benefits of this private retreat in the intimate setting of a Missionaries of Charity convent. I was very much looking forward to working in the sisters' soup kitchen that weekend as well.

Every one of Mother Teresa's convents is located in a poor, and often dangerous, location. This is so that the sisters can live among, and join in solidarity with, the world's "outcasts" — wherever in the world they live in great numbers. Mother Teresa was not oblivious to the very real dangers inherent in such places. She instructed her sisters to pray the Rosary when traveling the streets ministering to people. She told them to invoke the protective intercession of the Blessed Mother at all times.

In Harlem, the Missionaries of Charity offered to put me up at their convent's shelter for women. This meant that I would have a metal-framed bunk bed to sleep on — a big step up in comfort from the thin floor mats the sisters used. I would also have to find a way to sleep amid the cacophony of traffic, shouting, and pounding bass music that blared all through the night just outside our safe place. Add to that the sounds of my shelter-mates, and the aural assault was a far cry from the nighttime symphony of silence, crickets, and peepers so familiar to me in rural Connecticut.

I found the culture shock quite unsettling even though I knew, in part from Father Hardon's wise spiritual counsel, that hearing the world through the ears of the poor would do my soul as much good as seeing things through their eyes. In short, the brief Harlem experience gave me my first real taste of what the Missionaries of Charity willingly experience every day and every night of their lives.

So there I slept, or tried to, in a threadbare shelter filled with homeless women from all sorts of backgrounds and situations. Many of my neighbors seemed to toss and turn all night; others snored away the hours. In fact, thinking back, I did not get much sleep at all that weekend.

I recall beginning each morning feeling sore, exhausted, and humbled. Why humbled? Because I knew that the women waking up around me were deeply appreciative for the free, safe, and secure accommodations — while I was looking at the sleeping arrangements as something to be endured, even if with gratitude. I was fully cognizant of the difference between my perspective and that of the other women who found themselves in the shelter.

It was an interesting weekend, to say the least, and it involved me quite intimately in the work — and life — of the Missionaries of Charity and the poor they serve. Partaking in the routine of the sisters that weekend included attending daily Mass and praying with the sisters whenever the bell summoned us to the chapel. I also took meals with the sisters and assisted in the soup kitchen.

The sisters were always smiling, always cheerful. An unsuspecting outsider, I thought, would see no obvious signs of the austere life the Missionaries lived inside their convent. In fact, as I saw, the sisters own very close to nothing at all. Each member of the community in Harlem had use of one set of rosary beads, a prayer book, a toothbrush, a comb, two saris (so that one could be washed while one was worn), two sets of undergarments, one pair of sandals, the small crucifix pinned to their sari — and that's it. I noted that there are no mirrors at all in their convents. Life there is stripped to the bare essentials so that the Church's call to holiness can be answered without distraction.

While I don't consider myself someone inordinately preoccupied with vanity, I did miss having use of a mirror that weekend. But by the time I was ready to leave for home, my thoughts about that had changed. Mother Teresa, I learned, vehemently opposed the use of creature comforts in her convents. She considered modern conveniences — fans, air conditioning, hot water, carpeting, drapery, washing machines, and so on — luxuries. These, she said, the sisters could and should live without.

Mother Teresa and the sisters wholeheartedly lived and breathed their vows of poverty. Mother Teresa believed that they could not serve the poor properly if they did not live exactly as the poor themselves. In her marvelous wisdom, she also knew that voluntary poverty does not constrain; on the contrary, it liberates. It frees a person of attachments to, and care for, material things. Because of this, he or she can focus on what is truly essential: God and neighbor.

To this day I often find myself looking around my home, seeing so much stuff and wishing I could be free of at least some of it. I know that having fewer material possessions to worry about would help de-clutter my mind, allowing me to set my mind on Our Lord and the people he has placed with me and near me.

By their fruits

Father Hardon found me shortly after I arrived at the convent that Friday morning. With a smile on his face and a twinkle in his eye, he offered a little suggestion to help me settle in. "Don't be afraid," he said, "to roll up your sleeves."

Father John Hardon, SJ, my spiritual director, with my son Joseph at a retreat in Washington, DC

This, I knew, was his polite way of telling me to pitch in and help the sisters. I happily took the hint.

After making my way to the soup kitchen, I pitched in with the food-preparation process. Later, I "rolled up my sleeves" to help fill bowls and plates for the hundreds of hungry guests who came in for a hot meal. It was an extraordinary experience, one I'll never forget.

Also, after that weekend, I would never again look at a piece of imperfectly fresh fruit with disgust. Each day the women from the shelter, the sisters, and I prepared food for the afternoon and evening soup-kitchen meal from fruits and vegetables donated by local markets. The gifts were the stores' throwaways, most of the items being slightly spoiled or simply too far past the "sell-by" date to sell to paying customers. The sisters accepted every edible offering with great appreciation.

We sat at long tables piled high with produce of every variety, sorting the good from the bad, and the partially bad from the completely rotten. The good we put into big pots and bowls to be washed and served for dinner. The bad we tossed straight into trash cans placed at the ends of the tables. As for the food that was on the borderline between good and bad, the sisters instructed us to cut away the rotting parts and save whatever we could of the rest.

Sounds easy, right? Not so fast!

Being a mother of three children at that time, one concerned about both wastefulness and high prices, I prided myself on such frugal habits as getting the last little bit of peanut butter from what appeared to be an empty jar. I'm sure that growing up in a family of eight children had something to do with this trait. I was not one to waste food.

Well, I thought I was doing a pretty good job sorting and preparing the food for the shelter when a sister walked by and retrieved a rotten pear I'd just thrown out. She retrieved the pear from the garbage pail, walked over to me and pointed out a small unspoiled spot that could be eaten. She handed the pear back to me and continued walking past. I will never forget that moment as long as I live.

It was then that the total commitment of the Missionaries of Charity — sisters, brothers, and priests alike — hit home for me. In more than 120 countries around the world, in 517 missions, these workers in God's vineyard take other people's garbage and transform it into feasts for the hungry. They rely totally on God's providence to provide for all of their needs and the needs of the poor. And God provides: Mother Teresa's missionaries have never gone wanting for food — for themselves or for the poor they serve.

The lesson I learned from the sister retrieving the rotten pear from the trash reminds me of the times my family and I shared meals with Father Hardon. When we met him in Washington, DC, or in New York at various times, we often went off to talk over spiritual matters. His choice of restaurant was always McDonald's. I know it wasn't due to his preference of food, but rather the fact that Father did not want to eat anything too satisfying or too expensive in the spirit of poverty which he lived. My children didn't mind at all. They enjoyed occasional French fries or chicken nuggets. I'll always remember what he said to me when he saw my children leave behind a few stray French fries. "What would Mother Teresa say about wasting that food?" he would ask.

Now, back to the soup kitchen in Harlem: later on, the smells of fresh, hearty soup filled the convent's kitchen as supper bubbled up in large pots. Indeed, the enticing aroma wafted throughout the convent. Its delicious source would be a gift to the hungry of Harlem a little later that afternoon. Served along with the fruit salad made from the salvaged fruit, and some slightly stale bread and butter, the multi-course meal was truly a feast — one whose main ingredient was love.

Full bellies, peaceful hearts

When the droves of people came in for their daily hot meal, I witnessed God's power working in tangible ways. Gang members from opposite sides of the street (sworn enemies who defended unto death their turf in the dilapidated battlefield outside) came in to eat at the same tables at the same time. I had no idea what to expect. I watched with a keen eye as I manned my position near the pans of hot food and the stacked dinner plates, waiting to serve.

Within minutes, several guests began to bicker. A fight broke out. A Missionaries of Charity priest, small in stature, hurried toward the fracas and announced: "Gentlemen! We take our hats off when we pray." Amazingly, everyone quieted down. I don't think there was really an issue about hats, though. I think this wise priest knew exactly what he needed to say to bring God's peace.

The priest led the room in the Our Father, then said grace over the food. It seemed to me a minor miracle when even the hardened gang members settled down and began to line up for dinner in an orderly way.

I stood between a couple of the sisters as we dished out food and handed plates to the long line of hungry guests. I was told to heap the dishes high with food since this would most likely be the guests' only real meal that day. In fact, it might be the only thing they'd have to eat at all. Catching their eyes in mine was an indescribable experience, not easy for me to explain.

It was also an incredible sight observing the rough and scary gang members sitting with their families and so many other people. All ate together in the same room, plainly enjoying the banquet.

Mother Teresa taught her people well, I recall observing silently. How right I was! The sisters, brothers, and priests of the Missionaries of Charity have learned that an intense prayer life is essential to the success of their work. They depend on God for every single need. They are not social workers but rather "contemplatives in the heart of the world." They say this because they know that, without the kind of love that prayer makes possible, they would be "a resounding gong or a clashing cymbal" (1 Cor 13:1). Their prayers for the poor — said through the work of their hands as well as the lifting of their voices — clearly do change hearts.

I was in awe that weekend. I still am today.

+LDM   9th June,1989

Dear Donna,

Thank you very much for you
kind letter, prayers and
good wishes.

I am happy for the gift of
baby boy that God has given
you. He is a gift of God's
love for you.

Keep the joy of loving
Jesus in each other and
continue to share it with
your own.

God bless you
Me Teresa mc

Six

OF BABIES AND BOOKS

Every so often over the next few years, a question would pass through my mind: Who am I to receive the direct intercessory prayers of Mother Teresa for my children, born and unborn?

You see, unbeknownst to me, the baby residing in my womb — hidden from even his mother at the time that I stayed with the sisters in Harlem — would later be blessed by Mother Teresa. It happened a few months later, when I saw her in the Bronx. The Missionaries of Charity there invited my whole family to their convent while Mother Teresa was visiting.

When we arrived, Mother came over and tickled baby Joseph's chubby legs. I remember that he squealed in my arms as my other children surrounded the three of us. And I recall how happy Mother Teresa looked as she took Joseph from me and raised him up, rejoicing in the beauty of his new life.

I knew her joy to be genuine and heartfelt, for Mother Teresa and her sisters had prayed for me and Joseph during the pregnancy. It had been a precarious time for both of us, as I'd developed a heart condition requiring medication and close supervision by a team of doctors. In fact, I had seen her a few months earlier, when I was quite

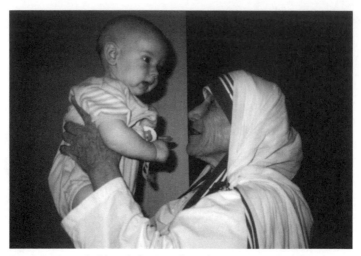

Mother Teresa holding baby Joseph at the convent in New Jersey.

obviously showing with Joseph. She'd placed a hand on my belly and prayed for both of us. So this was a precious moment indeed, watching a living saint jubilate over my infant son.

Now a young man, Joseph is a real gift to all who know him. He yearns for the truth, expresses concern whenever justice is on the line, and has a real heart for the poor and less fortunate. I suspect that Mother Teresa's prayers, along with my own before Jesus in the Blessed Sacrament during this pregnancy, had something to do with his inspiring spiritual development.

Interestingly enough, as a one-year-old baby, Joseph handed a beautiful rosary to Cardinal John O'Connor. It happened at St. Patrick's Cathedral, and it was linked to generous gestures from both Cardinal O'Connor and Mother Teresa.

The Archdiocese of New York had invited my family to a small gathering of Catholics in Manhattan one Sunday afternoon. On our way to the city, I felt inspired to stop at St. Joseph's Corner, the Catholic bookstore I owned at the time. I wanted to run in and get the best rosary I could find and present it to the cardinal. I chose a hand-carved, olive-wood rosary with a sterling-silver crucifix and medal. I prayed for the opportunity to arise if my wish accorded with God's will.

Evidently, God approved wholeheartedly. As Cardinal O'Connor approached us, I put the rosary in Joseph's hands and told him to give it to the man. "What's this?" said the cardinal as he accepted the gift from Joseph. "Why are you handing me these?" I explained about my little inspiration at St. Joseph's Corner. He smiled broadly. "It's just so interesting and providential that you should give me these," he said. "I just gave my rosary beads to Mother Teresa yesterday because she had just given hers away."

Today I find myself reflecting on this happy memory and thinking, *Who knows how long Cardinal O'Connor kept those beads before passing them along to someone else?* Only God and the recipient, I suppose. I always find it fascinating to see the Lord at work in these small yet profound ways — they seem to serve as signals of his presence.

Saved on the street

One time, when I was traveling to Rome to attend one of Blessed John Paul II's Masses, Father Hardon sent me on a mission. He wanted me to bring important papers to Cardinal Eduardo Pironio, who was then president of the Pontifical Council for the Laity. (Cardinal Pironio died in 1998; the cause for his beatification is underway.) The papers involved a group Father Hardon was forming called the Marian Catechists.

In retrospect, I can see that this 1988 trip with Joseph — preborn — touched my son's spirit. How could it not? We stayed with Blessed John Paul's beloved Polish nuns near the Vatican, received the Pope's blessing at the Mass, and were prayed over by Cardinal Pironio.

Around twenty years later, the intervention of Blessed Teresa saved my son's life. Most amazingly, it happened very close to the spot at which she had blessed Joseph in my womb. My mother's heart aches to retell this story, but, in the end, God gets the glory — so here goes.

One spring night, Joseph set out on foot with a group of his college buddies. They headed for the housing of some other friends who lived off-campus. Suddenly, a gang from the rough urban neighborhood surrounded the students. Most were able to get away, but, as Joseph fled, he sensed trouble behind him. He turned to see his instincts confirmed: One of his friends had not made a getaway. He stood alone against the attackers.

Joseph rushed back and pushed the lead aggressor off the terrified student, who ran away. Now Joseph was the target. The violent thugs repeatedly punched my son in the face. Joseph asked what they wanted. "My wallet?" he asked. "My shirt?" But it wasn't robbery that the gang had in mind. They just wanted to hurt someone. "Shut up," they told him, then warned him that if he fought back, they would use their weapons on him. They made it clear, in the harshest terms, that they weren't bluffing with their deadly threats.

Holding Joseph as Chaldea looks on; Mother Teresa squeezing Joseph's legs

Finally, the delinquents allowed Joseph to escape. He made it to a hospital, where he was examined, treated, and released. He had been pummeled without mercy, but, thanks be to God, his life had been spared. The injuries healed, and he got on with his beautiful life.

I knew in my heart that the Blessed Mother and Blessed Teresa had intervened that night to save my son, who had sacrificed his own safety to free a friend from danger. I recall thinking back to the two special times Mother Teresa had blessed Joseph so early in his life — before he was born and not long after — and knowing that more than coincidence was at work in his life.

Don't give up on my baby

A few years after Joseph's birth, Mother Teresa "prayed me through" another high-risk pregnancy, as well as some other spiritually exhausting circumstances.

Again and again, she taught me about the hidden, mysterious graces that can be found in suffering. More than once she told me, "You have come so close to Jesus on the cross that He can kiss you." More than once these words affected me intensely.

During my next pregnancy, I again developed serious complications. This time, in fact, it was even worse. Along with the continuing heart problem, I also hemorrhaged. My doctor ordered complete bed rest for almost the entire nine months, and I needed three times the dosage of heart medication I'd had with Joseph. (My doctor assured me that this would not harm my developing baby.)

Specifically, ten weeks into the pregnancy, my uterus hemorrhaged. The bleeding was profuse. My doctor told me to get off my feet immediately and remain on bed rest until the following day, when he would perform a sonogram to check on the baby. I had experienced three previous miscarriages, including one in which I barely escaped death because of severe hemorrhaging and complications. This time I was more deeply troubled than ever before over the thought of possibly losing another baby. I went straight to bed. I prayed. And, in the subsequent days and weeks, I went about following the doctor's orders without compromise.

During one office visit, my doctor told me that, based on my history and condition, he did not think this baby would make it. I wrote Mother Teresa and asked for her immediate prayers. I called my friends and family, pleading for their prayers as well. The following day, the sonogram revealed a tiny, ten-week-old baby with a beating heart. Thanks be to God!

I was told to go home and go straight back to bed. Just the thought of resting was strange. Most busy mothers rarely have time to nap, much less get a full night's sleep, and now I would be forced to. I had four active children at home, and now I wouldn't be able to keep up with them. The logistics in the household changed dramatically, as we now required a nurse to visit regularly and a home-health aide to come in every day to help with the care of the children and the house.

When I wasn't at the doctor's office, my time was spent lying on the couch or on my bed, caring for my family and running my household as best as I could while staying off my feet. My kids bustled around me, keeping me company, drawing me pictures, playing games, bringing me treats, and doing their homework.

The hemorrhaging continued, and I committed myself to staying still and waiting. I had to undergo many sonograms at various times throughout my pregnancy. Each one confirmed the hemorrhaging, as well as the beating of my baby's tiny heart. Those readings filled me with hope. Still, my baby's life always seemed in jeopardy.

Nor was this just the misperception of an overly worried mom. My doctor seemed intent on preparing me for the worst. "I almost wish you would hurry up and have that miscarriage," he told me one time. I suppose he figured a miscarriage would somehow save me from further suffering and anguish, but his words brought me no comfort. On the contrary, they pierced my heart like a sword. After all, this was the doctor who should have been preparing to deliver my baby in less than seven months.

The pregnancy seemed extraordinarily long. Sometimes I shed tears of frustration and concern. I cried out to God, asking for health for my baby. It wasn't easy for me to sit still, much less lie around.

I missed going to Mass and greatly appreciated the extraordinary ministers of holy Communion who brought the Body of Christ to my home. I also missed playing outside with Justin, Chaldea, Jessica, and Joseph — not to mention attending their activities at school, going for walks, and visiting family and friends. But I remained determined to do whatever it took and give up whatever I needed to in order to give my baby a fighting chance at life.

One day when I least expected it, an envelope turned up in my mailbox with the unmistakable Calcutta return-address stamp. "Mother Teresa is coming to my rescue!" I said to myself before praying, "Thank you, dear Lord!" The envelope had a small bulge in one spot. I opened it carefully, excited that word and gift had come from my dear friend, spiritual guide, and confidant. I read her words slowly, taking them straight to my heart.

> *"Do not be afraid. Just put yourself in the Hands of our Blessed Mother and let her take care of you. When you are afraid or sad or troubled just tell her so. She will prove Herself a Mother to you. Pray often: 'Mary, Mother of Jesus, make me alright'; 'Mary, Mother of Jesus, be a Mother to me now.' Enclosed is a Miraculous Medal. She has done wonders for others and she will do so for you too. Just trust and pray. I am praying for you and the baby."*

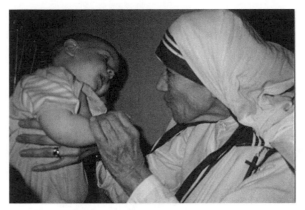

My son Joseph (in my arms) with Mother Teresa at a Missionary of Charity convent.

An indescribable peace came over me. I must have reread her letter a dozen times as I sat propped up on my living room couch. "Do not be afraid. Just put yourself in the Hands of our Blessed Mother and let her take care of you." These words echoed in my heart. This was indeed a letter I would cherish along with the others. Mother Teresa's words to me in this letter became a healing mantle that I wrapped around myself as I continued to implore the Blessed Mother for her intercession. "Mary, Mother of Jesus," I prayed, "be a Mother to me now."

After reading this letter many times over, I felt a strong confirmation that everything would be okay. How could it not? Mother Teresa had put in a good word for me to the Blessed Mother and her Son, Jesus. I had already been wearing a Miraculous Medal from Mother Teresa, but this one seemed even more special. She had sent it to me just for this pregnancy, and she was by this time my dear spiritual guide. To this day, I wear it constantly.

Mother Teresa's powerful prayers gave me much strength. I clung to the Blessed Mother, hung tightly to hope, and stayed still on my bed rest to preserve my baby's life. Finally, on July 25 that year (feast of St. James the Apostle, and the day before the feast of St. Anne and St. Joachim), Mary-Catherine Anne came into this world. Hallelujah! I sent Mother Teresa her birth announcement, and she rejoiced along with me, proclaiming, "Thank God for his great gift of Mary-Catherine Anne!" She handwrote these words on the birth announcement I had sent her.

It's no wonder this daughter of mine is such a great gift. She is sweetness personified and has a warm heart that always seems to be reaching out to someone. Those prayers from dear Mother Teresa surely must have given us all extra grace, piled high on top of the prayers I continued to get from my spiritual director, Father Hardon — who became Mary-Catherine's godfather. (Again: Hallelujah!)

Come to think of it, all five of my children have been changed by their nearness — direct and indirect — to Mother Teresa, Father Hardon, and other holy people who have been sent into our lives by the grace of God. Justin, Chaldea, Jessica, Joseph, and Mary-Catherine: I'm sure that their grace-filled brushes with spiritual greatness helped form all my children's consciences for the better — perhaps in ways they may not even be aware of.

From notes to books

I later understood another purpose for my staying put during this pregnancy. During this time, I began to write about motherhood. I felt inspired to jot down my thoughts and reflections as all of my motherly hormones were floating around my body. I guess our good Lord knew he couldn't get me to sit still long enough to write a book (or two or three!) with four active kids in the household. So he put me in a situation that kept me still and had me write.

I wrote a manuscript for expectant mothers, which I thought might be called *A Journey of Prayer as You Wait*. I envisioned the pregnancy as a journey — a virtual pilgrimage of faith, hope, and love to the day of the baby's birth. It became clear to me that a pregnancy is a perfect and distinctive nine-month "sabbatical" in which a mother can reflect and pray as her baby grows within. Pregnancies are a time of sacrifice as we give our bodies over to a new life growing within us, allowing the new life to make us sick in the morning and heavier than we'd like to be day by day. But they could also be thought of as an extended novena: nine months of prayer. As time went on, I decided to call this writing *Prayerfully Expecting: A Nine-Month Novena for Mothers-to-Be*.

As I shared everything with Mother Teresa, I also felt inspired to share my writings and my manuscripts. As busy as she was with world affairs and caring for the poorest of the poor, she took the time to read my work and to encourage me to continue to write, telling me that mothers really needed it. She wrote in a letter: "Your two books on young mothers and expectant mothers are much needed. Yes, you may use some of the things I said on motherhood and family. I pray it does much good." She always encouraged me.

Another time she said: "God has given you many gifts; make sure you use them for the glory of God and the good of the people. You will then make your life something beautiful for God. You were created to be holy. I assure you of my prayers and hope you pray for me also. Keep the love of Jesus ever burning in your heart, and share this joy with others. My gratitude is my prayer for you that you may grow in the love of God through your beautiful thoughts of prayer that you write and thus share with others."

Mother Teresa's continual encouragement and God's grace gave me the strength and inspiration to continue putting pen to paper and fingers to keys. "It is a gift from God to be used for His glory," she wrote, and I wasn't about to disagree with Mother Teresa. I continued writing and speaking about God's life-changing ways, trusting him to give me the words. I was humbled and overjoyed to receive Mother Teresa's foreword for my book *Prayerfully Expecting,* as well as her endorsements ahead of time for my other books as they came out.

And come out they did. Being required to stay put for so long, and having all of those wonderful motherly hormones in my body, I found time to write several "motherly manuscripts." I wrote extensively about the necessity of prayer for survival for mothers and families. I praised mothers and encouraged them, pointing out that their vocations were amazing, sublime, and rooted in love — and so should also be rooted in prayer.

Motherhood was not just changing diapers and keeping up with the demands of housework; it was raising little saints to populate heaven. These manuscripts were read by Mother Teresa and looked over by her spiritual director. They went on to become books in later years, when I had time to pursue publishing and offer my thoughts to a wider audience. A few of the manuscripts written during my pregnancy with Mary-Catherine have yet to be published. All in God's timing.

I could never have imagined that I would be writing these books to give encouragement and inspiration to others. After all, I was inundated with the care of my own family, with all the joys and challenges of this massive responsibility. Later on, I would face larger trials and tribulations, always coupled with God's grace.

A ministry is born

With the publishing of my books, a ministry to mothers, women, and families began — one I neither expected nor had any intention of starting. It unfolded as I was speaking with a priest I knew, Father Paul Murphy, about my first book coming out for Catholic mothers. He invited me to be a speaker at a day of recollection he was planning for his parish. As we sat and talked at his rectory in Ridgefield, Connecticut, I heard Our Lord telling me in an unmistakable way that I would be doing this continuously to help and encourage mothers, women, and families. To this time I'd been content to write. Now, I knew, more was being asked of me.

I remember at my first book signing, at my own parish, I sat at a table in my church hall and signed away. At one point, I picked my head up from my ceaseless signing for a second to discover that there was a line of people waiting for an autographed book that went clear across the room. I was amazed. The next book signing at my local Borders bookstore brought many people too. The manager, Matt, told me afterward that it was "unheard of!" He had never seen so many books sell at a book signing before. The wonderful part for me was that the people who came up to my table were quietly telling me about themselves, their woes, and asking for prayers. I was all ears.

One couple told me about a relative with a brain tumor and pleaded for prayers. Everyone had a story, and everyone wanted prayer. I felt a burden placed on my heart right then to pray for all of these people. And I do pray for them all.

My first speaking event after my book was released was in a parish in West Hartford, Connecticut. This talk was addressed to women of every walk of life and was called "Woman's Call to Prayer." It was received very well. At one point about halfway through it, though, I spotted a woman crying. My initial feeling was of sorrow. Not even half a second went by and I sensed that it was okay: she was fine, not to worry. Our Lord was working on her heart.

A couple of weeks later, I gave my talk at the Ridgefield event, and more than one hundred women showed up. It was received well, and I was happy to offer words of inspiration by God's grace. A couple of days later I received a card in the mail from my friend Mary Frank, who had attended the event. She complimented me on the presentation and told me that all of the women who surrounded her in the audience were brought to tears by my words. I was shocked. I hadn't seen that, but it brought to mind my talk in West Hartford just a couple of weeks before in which I saw that woman cry in the audience.

I called Mary on the phone to talk about it. She explained what she experienced, and I knew then that God was using me to reach these people. He was inspiring them and working on their hearts. The words touched a chord in them and nourished their souls. This was a surprise to me. It had all unfolded by God's grace and a desiring heart on my part to do his will.

God does not disappoint. Because I had witnessed the tears at my first talk — and because the tears of others were brought to my attention by my friend Mary at the second talk — I became very aware of God working in this way at all my talks and book signings. At each and every one, at least one person was brought to tears. This was an aspect of my ministry that I have kept quiet up until now.

One of the most rewarding aspects of this ministry is the correspondence I've come to share, thanks to modern technology, with people all over the world. I am in touch with countless people who contact me for prayer, advice, and conversation. They tell me that my books have helped them a great deal. Their words remind me that we all make up the Body of Christ. When one member suffers, we all suffer. When one rejoices, we all rejoice.

I believe Blessed Teresa of Calcutta suffers and rejoices with us, too. To find out how and why I've come to believe this, read on.

MISSIONARIES OF CHARITY
54A A.J.C. BOSE ROAD
CALCUTTA — 700016

Sept   1989

Dear Donna,

Thank you for your letter and assurance of prayers.

Since every good desire comes from God Himself, Jesus must have kindled this desire to console Him in all who suffer. He said " I looked for one to comfort me, but found none". Be that one to comfort Him, through your prayers and good works.

To know how He wants you to serve Him concrete-ly, pray for the light to know His will, the love to accept it and the courage to do it. You are in our prayers.

God bless you
lee Teresa mc

Seven

"I Thirst"

Through Mother Teresa and the Missionaries of Charity, I learned much about these two poignant and profound words: "I thirst."

These two words mark every chapel in every Missionaries of Charity convent in the world. The words are painted on the wall beside the crucifix and altar, usually right next to the tabernacle. They stand out from the otherwise bare walls of the simple chapels that I have visited.

Throughout Christian history, Christians have meditated on Jesus speaking the very words "I thirst" while dying on the cross (Jn 19:28). They have also considered how, elsewhere in Scripture, Jesus expresses his thirst for mankind and mankind's thirst (whether recognized or unrecognized) for him.

Jesus meets a Samaritan woman fetching water from Jacob's well. He confronts her with his love, expressing his "thirst" in direct statements about her life. At the time, it was taboo on social as well as religious grounds for a Jewish man to speak to a Samaritan woman. Nevertheless, Jesus enters into dialogue with the woman, telling her that the water from the well will never quench the thirst of her heart — but the "living water" that he alone can give will become in those who receive it "a spring of water gushing up to eternal life" (Jn 4:14).

After much discussion and initial attempts to escape Jesus' questioning, the woman accepts the "living water" and is healed by Jesus' thirst. She leaves her jar at the well and becomes a missionary, running to bring this Good News to her Samaritan people. Members of her community run out to meet Jesus. As soon as they do, they believe in him.

I am also reminded of Jesus speaking about our thirst for his love in John 7:37-38. He said, "Let anyone who is thirsty come to me, and let the one who believes in me drink. As the scripture has said, 'Out of the believers heart shall flow rivers of living water.'"

The school of Mother Teresa

Before getting to know Mother Teresa, I had an inkling that Jesus' words "I thirst" were profound, meaning many things on many levels. But now I cannot hear those Gospel words without recalling how intensely they affected Mother Teresa in some very particular ways. In fact, these words really form the heart of Blessed Teresa's ministry; they sum up her own thirst to satiate Jesus' thirst for souls in an intimate way. This is why the words are prominently displayed in Missionaries of Charity chapels. Also, Blessed Teresa included in the constitutions of the Missionaries of Charity some stirring words about Jesus' thirst, along with directives for the sisters on how to respond to his thirst:

> *"I thirst," Jesus said on the cross when he was deprived of every consolation and left alone, despised and afflicted in body and soul. As Missionaries of Charity, we are*

called to quench the infinite thirst of Christ — God made Man who suffered, died, yet rose again and is now at the right hand of his Father as well as fully present in the Eucharist, making intercession for us by: a deep life of prayer, contemplation, and penance; accepting all suffering, renunciation, and even death; as means to understanding better our special call to love and serve Christ in the distressing disguise of the poor.

Every time I saw her, I noticed how powerfully the words "I thirst" echoed in Blessed Teresa's soul. Her desire to satiate Jesus' thirst for love was clearly evident in her dealings with others, when she received holy Communion and retreated deeply into recollection, and when she knelt before him really present in the Blessed Sacrament. I was profoundly edified to witness these sights, knowing that she was driven in all she did by an unquenchable desire to respond to Jesus' words "I thirst."

In the "school of Mother Teresa," I learned that, in addition to Jesus thirsting for our love, he wants us to thirst and hunger for him. We read in the Psalms, "My soul thirsts for God, for the living God. When shall I come and behold the face of God? My tears have been my food day and night, while people say to me continually, 'Where is your God?' " (42:2–3).

Mother Teresa never ceased to remind us, by word and example, that we can let Jesus feed our hunger and quench our thirst every day at Holy Mass. We can ask him to come to us in a "spiritual communion" when we are not able to get to Mass because of sickness, infirmity, care of family, or other situations. As we nourish ourselves with the Bread of Life, we grow in faith and receive much grace to aid us on our journey.

Prison breakthrough

I'm often amazed at how Jesus shows us his thirst for our love in real-world situations. Let me give one example.

I know a woman who went through what she thought was "hell on earth" when her nineteen-year-old son was arrested. Her son was a decent young man who held a job, was good to his family, and never got in trouble. But one night, due to an unfortunate series of events, he put himself in the wrong place at the wrong time: he got involved in a fight at a party. He was sentenced to serve six months in prison.

This mom told me that at the time of her son's judgment in court, she was inconsolable. She had to turn away, unable to bear the sight of her beloved son being taken away in clanging shackles by armed guards.

A few months later, both mother and son had a completely different outlook. The mom remembers her first visit to her son at prison very vividly. Before prison, her son was usually fashionably dressed, but he met his mom in white prison garb, a reminder of freedoms removed. Her son handled his sentence well, though. Mixed in with dangerous criminals, he said to his mom, "These people have made mistakes, but I haven't met anyone I'm afraid of."

Her son had to wait three weeks for the privilege of a pencil, then another three for a piece of paper — rewards for good prison behavior. After two and a half months, this young man was taken to a new cell and had to pass through the outside courtyard with the guards. He tried to slow down his pace a bit to breathe in the fresh air of the outdoors, which he had missed for more than two months.

The mom explained to me, "As bad as this is, I am strengthened by it." She said she sees her son as "a different kid for this." Being in prison has caused him to stop and think, to slow down and appreciate what he had. It gave him the opportunity to actually pray. He began answering letters from his parish priest, something his mom said he would never have bothered to do before this sudden interruption in his life.

This son also spoke to his father while in prison, and this alone was a minor miracle. Before his prison sentence, he had barely spoken to his dad in years; never mind that they lived under the same roof. His dad visited him in jail every night, and they talked face-to-face through a glass window.

Mail poured in from parishioners to this young man, and he began to feel genuinely loved. His healing process began.

Meanwhile, his mom told me that sometimes she found it difficult to wait hours to see her son because of prison rules. She was surrounded by the other mothers and grandmothers who were also waiting to visit loved ones. Not accustomed to hanging out with such a vast group of culturally and racially diverse people, she thought, "I am better than this." She didn't want to have to wait — she didn't want to be with all of these people she didn't know and with whom she felt she couldn't relate about a single thing. She would fidget, pace, and mumble little complaints.

MOTHER TERESA AND ME

Her attitude began to change when one day a little Hispanic woman came over and said, "You'll be all right." And she was. She was more than all right as she pondered how her son's punishment had changed her family for the better. She was also thankful for the woman who'd ventured over to her to help put her mind at ease.

Perhaps it was the combination of prison time and loving expressions that helped the young man and his mother heal and change into better, more loving people. And perhaps Jesus' thirst for their love had something to do with the happy outcome.

Jesus thirsts for our love. Are we willing to quench his thirst by giving our love and care to others — love that can transform souls, just as the priest, family, parishioners, and fellow visitors did in this story?

Mother Teresa said: "Jesus is God, therefore his love, his thirst is infinite. He, the creator of the universe, asked for the love of his creatures. He thirsts for our love. These words: 'I thirst' — do they echo in our souls?" These are amazing words for us to ponder in our own hearts.

Help, not pity

"The poor do not need our compassion or pity; they need our help," Blessed Teresa often said. "What they give to us is more than we give to them."

Although her work revolved around caring for the poor, Mother Teresa grounded herself in prayer to be able to do the work. Still today, prayer fuels the fire that burns in the hearts of the Missionaries of Charity, giving them the strength they need to serve the poor. Sometimes they pray while on their knees; other times, they "pray" by extending their loving hands to Jesus in the poor, sick, lonely, and dying.

To pray with Blessed Teresa and the sisters was a real privilege for me. Their prayers were voiced from pure hearts; their singing was angelic. The atmosphere in the convents encouraged me to approach the mystery of God in a way I never had before. I quickly became consumed by the air of prayer that enveloped me within those walls.

The secret to the power of the sisters' prayer, I realized, is their complete trust in God. With contrite, humble hearts, they reach up to the Almighty in total abandonment to his love. I don't think my transformation was unique among lay people who have had a chance to spend time with the Missionaries of Charity. They lead by example, and I learned by watching and imitating them. I learned volumes about prayer just by observing their bowed heads and clasped hands, their deep recollection after receiving Jesus in holy Communion, and their unshakable focus when they went before Jesus in Eucharistic Adoration.

Every time I joined in their prayer, I felt enveloped in their peace. Other times, their laughter, smiles, and tender acts of love for orphans, the dying, and the poor reminded me that their lives are both active and contemplative — as my life should be, along with the lives of most other Catholics.

I also recall many instances when Father Hardon was with Mother Teresa at the convents and in the chapels. To see these two holy souls conversing was extremely edifying. Their deep friendship, welded through their common faith in Jesus Christ, was so evident.

I find it interesting that Our Lord put Father Peter Towsley in my life, too, someone who also was linked in the marvelous Catholic connection of two of the saints I was privileged to know. Father Towsley also had occasion to witness Father Hardon and Mother Teresa together and was similarly moved by the sight. "They were like two children playing in God's garden," Father Towsley told me, referring to their easy repartee. "It was as if," he added, "beams of light flowed from the two of them."

"Joy is a net to catch souls," Blessed Teresa often said. These people were perfect examples to emulate. They were overflowing with joy and God's love.

"Behold your mother"

To answer God's call, Mother Teresa kept herself closely connected with the Blessed Mother. Jesus and Mary are inseparable, she stressed. Mother Teresa was very cognizant of the fact that, when Jesus hung from the cross, he presented us with his Mother: "Here is your mother," or, in some translations, "Behold your mother." It was only after that that he said, "I am thirsty," or "I thirst."

The Marian dimension of Christian prayer was central to Mother Teresa's prayer life. Just like Blessed John Paul II, she had a deep love for and intimate relationship with the Blessed Mother; we can say that she lived under Mary's mantle. Not only did she pray to the Blessed Mother seeking her help; she was also consecrated to her. She put her trust and confidence in Mary, and believed that Mary was truly present in her life. She actually abandoned her life into Mary's hands and heart, believing that

Mary would take care of all her needs and the needs of the poor. Who could understand us and know all of our needs better than the Mother of God?

Just as Blessed John Paul II was a great fan of St. Louis de Montfort and his formula for a consecration to Mary, Mother Teresa was as well. She encouraged others to get close to Our Lady too, believing that a healthy devotion to the Blessed Mother was essential to a committed Christian life. By placing herself totally in Mary's hands, Mother Teresa was being faithful to Jesus, as is illustrated in the Scriptures, "Do whatever he tells you" (Jn 2:5). This, of course, is what Mary said to the wine stewards during the wedding at Cana. Then followed Our Lord's first public miracle.

Mother Teresa was in constant communication with the Blessed Mother. She and her entire order prayed the Rosary daily. They wore a rosary at their waist as part of their religious habit, and rosary beads were often in Mother Teresa's hands as well. I saw her fingering her rosary on many occasions, moving her fingers from one bead to the next as she whispered her prayers. You knew that she was praying the Rosary even though she was often involved with the task at hand at the same time. Being with her on those occasions brought me a sense of deep peace. I could feel Mother Teresa's devotion and even the communion of the two: the Blessed Mother and Blessed Teresa.

Mother Teresa said: "Every holy Communion fills us with Jesus, and we must, with Our Lady, go in haste to give him to others. He made himself the Bread of Life so that we, too, like Mary, become full of Jesus. We, too, like her, must haste to give him to others. We, too, like her, serve others."

This was the crux of Blessed Teresa's life work. She acknowledged Jesus truly present in the Eucharist and also in the poor and those in need. She modeled herself after the Blessed Mother so that she, too, could bring Jesus to others as Mary did. Mother Teresa said that the Blessed Mother was the first missionary of charity, meaning that she was the first to receive Jesus physically and then carry Jesus to those who needed him most.

Express novenas

One time Mother Teresa said, "Whenever I need a special favor, I do an Express Novena." An Express Novena is nine Memorares in a row.

THE MEMORARE

Remember, O most gracious Virgin Mary, that never was it known that anyone who fled to your protection, implored your help, or sought your intercession was left unaided. Inspired with this confidence, I fly unto you, O Virgin of Virgins, my Mother; to you do I come, before you I stand, sinful and sorrowful. O Mother of the Word Incarnate, despise not my petitions, but in your mercy hear and answer me. Amen.

Mother Teresa gave an example of one of the positive outcomes from the Express Novena (or Memorare Novena). "In 1983, one of our Superior Sisters had gotten sick in East Berlin," she said. Mother Teresa had to appoint a replacement who could handle the communist government. The sister whom they appointed as a successor for East Berlin needed a visa to travel. Mother Teresa gathered her nuns and started praying the Express Novena. On the eighth Memorare, the phone rang. It was a communist official stating that it would be six months until they would receive the visa. After the ninth prayer, Mother Teresa started the novena again in thanksgiving, even though things were still looking grim. On the eighth Memorare the second time, the telephone rang again. This time, it was a communist official calling. He announced, "You will have your visa immediately!"

I have used Mother Teresa's method of praying a Memorare Novena often; I'm always thankful that I can have recourse to Mary in this way, too. Father Hardon prayed the Memorare Novena as well. We know we are in good company when we pray in this manner.

I wonder if we underestimate the Blessed Mother's power. One time, a friend called me in need of prayer and advice. She was enduring heartache because of family dynamics. She was facing a huge predicament and didn't quite know how to handle it. She only knew that she needed powerful prayer to thwart a serious crisis. I offered her prayer and a listening ear. I also suggested a Memorare Novena to the Blessed Mother because of her dire need. In other words, for lack of better terms, we wanted the Blessed Mother to move fast. Much to my friend's surprise, she received her miracle immediately after praying this novena.

I have seen this happen on many occasions. Of course, when we pray, we ask God for his holy will in our lives, and we should only expect what he wants for us. When our prayers are not answered in the manner in which we had hoped, we should remain in prayer and trust in God's perfect outcome. St. John Vianney said, "If you invoke the Blessed Virgin when you are tempted, she will come at once to your help, and Satan will leave you." These are powerful words for us to ponder and all the more reason to call upon the Blessed Mother in every necessity.

The Missionaries of Charity sisters in Port-au-Prince, Haiti, were inundated with caring for the injured and dying people in one of the areas worst affected by the earthquake of January 2010. When one of the terrifying, violent after-tremors struck, the sisters crowded into their little chapel and prayed. A statue of the Blessed Mother behind the altar that normally faced the congregation, slowly moved around, as the room shook until the figure faced the tabernacle, as if praying to her Son along with the Sisters. The aftershock stopped without causing any more damage or loss of life. The Sisters were so moved by what they felt was a miraculous act of mercy and love from the Blessed Mother that they cried as they recounted this story to my friend.

Medals and miracles

Mother Teresa gave blessed Miraculous Medals to everyone she met. (At least this is what I observed every time I was with her.) Miraculous Medals, known to win extraordinary graces for those who wear them and who pray for Mary's intercession and help, were first intro-duced to St. Catherine Laboure in 1830.

St. Catherine received visions from the Blessed Mother at the motherhouse of the Daughters of Charity of Saint Vincent de Paul in Paris. She was told by Mary to have the medals made. At first they were called the Medal of the Immaculate Conception. In 1832 the medals were struck with the approval of the archbishop and distributed throughout Paris. The words "O Mary, conceived without sin, pray for us who have recourse to you" were inscribed around the image of Mary. Almost immediately, the blessings and graces that the Blessed Mother had promised rained down on all who were wearing the medal.

The Miraculous Medal devotion spread with incredible speed and fervor as the graces manifested as miracles of peace, health, and prosperity. People began to call the medal the "Miraculous Medal," and in 1836 a canonical inquiry declared Catherine's apparitions authentic.

I really admired Mother Teresa's unshakable faith, but I also loved her feisty attitude. One time in 1971, Mother Teresa went to see a property that she hoped could house her novitiate in Dublin, Ireland. The real estate agent told her that it was for sale for £9,000. Mother Teresa told the realtor that she could pay only £6,000, thanked her for her time, and went on her way.

As she was leaving the property, Mother Teresa tossed a Miraculous Medal into the garden. Shortly afterward, Mother Teresa was given a donation of £5,995. The same day she received the donation, the real estate agent called to tell Mother Teresa that the owner of the property was willing to sell it for £6,000 in order to have a "house full of love."

Father Hardon told me the story about how the Miraculous Medal changed his life. He described the incident as "one of the most memorable experiences" he ever had. He said that, in the fall of 1948, a year after his ordination, a Vincentian priest came to speak to the young Jesuit priests. The visiting priest encouraged the Jesuits to enroll themselves in the Confraternity of the Miraculous Medal. Father Hardon recalled the Vincentian priest's words to them. "Fathers, the Miraculous Medal works," said the Vincentian. "Miracles have been performed by Our Lady through the Miraculous Medal."

Father Hardon admitted that he was not impressed by what the priest told him. He said that he was not "the medal-wearing kind of person," and did not even own a Miraculous Medal. He thought about it and figured it didn't cost anything, so he would put his name on the list to receive the leaflet of prayers of enrollment. A couple of weeks later, he received the leaflet and put it into his Divine Office prayer book. Then he forgot about it.

Four months later, Father Hardon was assigned to assist the chaplain at the St. Alexis Hospital in Cleveland, Ohio. Each day Father Hardon received a long list of the Catholics being admitted and did his best to visit each one. One day a nine-year-old boy was admitted to the hospital. He had suffered severe brain damage and a fractured skull after a sledding accident. By the time Father Hardon visited the boy, he had been in a coma for ten days, with no speech or any voluntary movements. The boy was diagnosed with permanent and inoperable brain damage and was not given much hope of surviving. Father Hardon blessed the boy and tried to console his parents. As he started to leave the boy's hospital room, a thought came to him. "That Vincentian priest," he recalled. "He told us, 'The Miraculous Medal works.' This can be a test of its alleged miraculous powers!"

He couldn't find a Miraculous Medal anywhere. He persisted and was able to acquire one through the nursing sisters at the hospital. He also had to find some sort of necklace to put around the boy's neck, as Our Lady's instructions called for wearing the medal around the neck. The sisters found a length of blue ribbon. Father Hardon said he felt a bit silly using a blue ribbon, but it did the trick. He blessed the medal, and the boy's father held the leaflet up for the prayers of investiture. Father Hardon recalled: "No sooner did I finish the prayer of enrolling the boy in the Confraternity than he opened his eyes for the first time in almost two weeks. He saw his mother and said, 'Ma, I want some ice cream.'"

The boy proceeded to talk with his parents. Everyone was amazed; someone ran to get the doctor. He examined the boy, and based on his findings, he said the young patient was well enough to eat. A series of x-rays showed that the brain damage had completely healed. More tests were administered over the following three days. All of them came back negative — no brain damage at all. The boy was released from the hospital and went home with his elated parents.

Father Hardon told me the experience changed his life profoundly. "The wonders the Blessed Mother performs, provided we believe, are extraordinary," he said. Needless to say, Father Hardon went on to promote the Blessed Mother's power and the Miraculous Medal with great zeal for the rest of his life.

A woman I know was suffering from breast cancer, and my family prayed for her every day. We were happy that her lumpectomy and subsequent treatments went well, and she was given a very good long-term prognosis. About a year later, however, her doctor told her that her cancer had returned, and she would have to have a full mastectomy. She was not Catholic, but at that point I felt inspired to give her a blessed Miraculous Medal, which she told me she began to wear.

Very shortly afterward, further testing revealed that her cancer was totally gone. There was no need for surgery. I attribute this turn of events to the Blessed Mother and her Miraculous Medal.

I have taken up the task of giving out blessed Miraculous Medals to all I meet at my retreats, speaking events, and book signings. I tell each person, as I hand over a medal, that I am carrying on Mother Teresa's tradition. I also give them a leaflet explaining the medal and its benefits. People have later written to me to tell me about the amazing things that have occurred after they started wearing the medals. It's not something to be superstitious about. Miraculous Medals are considered a sacramental of the Church.

Just like Blessed Teresa, we are all called to follow in Our Lord's footsteps in search of souls. Following her example, we can listen with our hearts to his voice beckoning us to quench his thirst. Mother Teresa urges us to root ourselves in the Mass and in prayer — ideally prayer before Jesus exposed in the Blessed Sacrament — and carry Jesus' light to others, especially to those most in need. In so doing, we will be satiating Jesus' thirst.

+LDM

7th March 1989

Dear Donna,

Thank you for the beautiful the way of the Cross
you sent me. My gratitude is my prayer for you
that you may grow in the love of God through
your beautiful thoughts of prayer you write and
thus share with others.

God has given you many gifts - make sure you
use them for the glory of God and the good of
the people. You will then make your life something beautiful for God. You have been created
to be Holy.

I assure you of my prayers and I hope you pray
for me also.

Keep the joy of loving Jesus ever burning in
your heart and share this joy with others.

God bless you
M. Teresa mc

Eight

THE POOREST OF THE POOR

Who are the poorest of the poor? Mother Teresa answered this question many times.

Today, the poor are hungry for bread and rice, and also for love and the living word of God. The poor are thirsty for water but also for peace, truth, and justice. The poor are homeless, in need of a shelter made of bricks, and also for a joyful heart that understands, covers, and loves. The poor are naked, in need of clothes and also for human dignity and compassion for the naked sinner. They are sick, in need of medical care and also for that gentle touch and a warm smile.

The "shut-in," the unwanted, the unloved, the alcoholics, the dying destitute, the abandoned and the lonely, the outcasts and the untouchables, the leprosy sufferers, all those who are a burden to human society, who have lost all hope and faith in life, who have forgotten how to smile, who have lost the sensibility of the warm hand touch of love and friendship, they look to us for comfort. If we turn our back on them, we turn it on Christ, and at the hour of our death we shall be judged if we have recognized Christ in them, and on what we have done for and to them, there will only be two ways, "come" or "go." (Mother Teresa: A Complete Authorized Biography, *Harper One, 1998)*

What Christian could hear those words and not be challenged to do more for the poor?

Mother Teresa's actions spoke even louder than her words. We know she devoted her entire ministry, at least fifty years of her life, to caring for the poorest of the poor. The poor whom she came into contact with were in worse than dire straights. Some of them were dying in the streets, never having known the shelter of a roof over their heads. The poor for whom Blessed Teresa cared sometimes were infected with maggots or covered with leprosy. She put herself in harm's way of all kinds of diseases and illnesses.

Mother Teresa often said that we must seek to understand the poor. We don't have to run off to Calcutta to encounter the poor. They exist in our own neighborhoods. The poor in our own areas may not have leprosy. They may not be homeless. But they may suffer from what Mother Teresa considers to be a worse disease — the disease of loneliness or of being unloved. "There are many kinds of poverty." she had said. "Even in countries where the economic situation seems to be a good one, there are expressions of poverty hidden in a deep place, such as the tremendous loneliness of people who have been abandoned and who are suffering."

Mother Teresa was upset about the imbalance of wealth in our world. She explained that wealth is not only property and money, but our attachment to these things and our abuse of them. "When things become our masters, we are very poor," she had said. "As long as there are rich people who commit excess and do not use things according to the mind of God, there will be poverty in the world."

When the rich decide to help the poor by donating something, Mother Teresa lamented that it was often expired foods and unwanted clothing. "We treat the poor like they are a garbage can," she said. She also pointed out that the most valuable thing we can give the poor is our time.

When Mother Teresa counseled us to take care of the poor who reside in our own homes, she wasn't talking about homeless persons we have taken in. She meant that there may be someone in our family who feels neglected or unloved. We need to be sure that their needs are seen to before rushing off to help the poor outside the doors of our homes.

Mother Teresa spoke often about Jesus coming to us in "the distressing disguise of the poorest of the poor." And she believed that material poverty isn't always the worst kind of want.

Mother Teresa grabbing my arm in New York after Mass, expressing delight that I became a lay Missionary of Charity.

I had an unforgettable experience with a woman whose name I don't know. I don't know where she was from originally or what kind of physical sickness she was suffering from. All I know is that I met her when I went into a local nursing home one day years ago. It was something I felt called to do — visit the lonely and sick. I was also an extraordinary minister of Holy Communion for the sick, and because of this, I frequently visited hospitals and nursing homes. Sometimes I brought my children along to help bring cheer to the patients and residents.

On this particular day, I was by myself. I walked down the corridor and was passing a room when an elderly woman who was lying in her bed caught my attention. I stopped and decided to go in to see her. I asked her if she wanted a visit. She expressed such happiness at the thought of it. I went in and sat in a chair beside her bed in her dimly lit room. I began to talk to her softly. She asked if I could please straighten her blankets and fluff up her pillow, which I did.

As we talked, I took her hand in mine. She then asked if I would rub her back for a moment, so I reached over and rubbed her back. She struggled to find words to express herself. She appeared to be overcome with joy and told me that she had never in her life felt as "satisfied" as she did at that very moment. Right then, when I looked into her eyes, I saw Jesus. I was certain that I had encountered him in this woman.

Jesus with a garbage bag

My parish priest, Father Mike, once shared an experience with me about meeting Jesus in the distressing disguise of the poorest of the poor. Before his ordination, when he was in his early twenties, he was raised in a prayerful atmosphere by his parents on Cape Cod. At that time, Father Mike participated in a Catholic pilgrimage and felt a spiritual awakening that he described as an "incredible, grace-filled experience." He felt God working in his life as he began discerning a vocation to the priesthood. He shared thoughts about his spirituality with his parents. His mother encouraged him to keep a journal. She said: "Write these things down now. With age comes wisdom, and God may have a lesson for you in the future."

Life went on, and Father Mike kept busy, too busy to go out and buy a journal. He began to participate in daily Mass, pray the Rosary regularly, and fast. Grace was unfolding in his life. One day he was driving down Main Street in Hyannis, Massachusetts, when he came upon a disheveled-looking woman. She was gesturing to him, so he pulled over to the side of the road.

She appeared to be homeless. She was overweight, missing several teeth, and carrying a black plastic garbage bag. She told Father Mike that her name was Mary Louise and that she needed a ride. She looked harmless enough, so Father Mike was willing to help her out. "My heart went out to her," he said. Mary Louise directed him to her apartment, which was in a subsidized housing complex. He decided to walk in with her to help her with her belongings.

He found her apartment to be "dingy, smelly, and depressing." Flies were buzzing around, and dirty dishes were strewn all over the apartment. What immediately caught his eye, though, were black garbage bags plastered all over the ceiling. Mary Louise quickly instructed Father Mike to keep his voice low. She thought that there might be microphones hidden all about, but the garbage bags would block any possible hidden cameras from taping her. She was obviously suffering from paranoid schizophrenia or some other mental illness.

Looking around a bit more closely, Father Mike noticed many statues of the Blessed Mother and St. Joseph, along with holy pictures, crucifixes, and other Catholic devotionals. "She clung to God," Father Mike surmised. They prayed together, and Father Mike's heart began to melt. He was overcome with compassion and truly envisioned Mary Louise as "Jesus in disguise."

Father Mike began to think about the possibility of joining the Franciscan order. He would see Mary Louise periodically around town and regularly at Mass. He continued to give her rides and brought her groceries at times. One day, after receiving holy Communion, when all was quiet in the church, Father Mike distinctly heard the words, "You will keep a journal."

The voice was audible. "It was not a suggestion," he said; he heard it as if coming from the authority of the Father. An extremely peaceful feeling came over him, and he felt aware of a mission that he was being given. He would be sure to buy a journal right after Mass.

As he got up to leave after the final blessing, he heard another voice. This time it said, "Michael!" The voice beckoned him with urgency. Again he heard, "Michael!" He wanted to leave the church to go on his mission for the journal, but he turned around — and there was Mary

Louise. Father Michael took a deep breath, putting aside some initial feelings of being a bit inconvenienced, recognizing that there is "always a grace" for him when he could help Mary Louise. She gave him a hug and asked, "Can you give me a ride?" Running through his mind was the fact that he was supposed to be on his way to the local department store on a "mission from God" to buy that journal.

He took another deep breath, smiled, and said, "Sure." Mary Louise then informed him that she had to get her belongings that she had left in the church. She ran to get her stuff and scurried back with the familiar black garbage bag. Father Mike took the load from her and opened the hatchback of his Honda Civic.

"Oh no, Michael," she said. "I wouldn't put my things in the back." She opened the front passenger door, plopped herself down on the seat of the car, and asked Father Mike to pass her the garbage bag. As he did, a pungent stench emanated from the bag's opening. Mary Louise put the bag between her legs, squeezing it as if to guard it. Mary Louise said she wanted to be dropped off at the Cape Cod shopping mall. On the way there, she babbled incoherently, her eyes darting all around. As they approached the mall, Father Mike began to feel relieved and excited. Finally he would be dropping Mary Louise off so he could buy his journal.

"Do you keep straw from the manger?" Mary Louise randomly asked, as her eyes darted about. "My father told me to always put straw under the mattress, and you will then be financially set for life and have good luck." Father Mike started to ponder the odd statement, but his thoughts quickly returned to his need to get to the store for his journal.

"Wait a minute," Mary Louise suddenly interjected. "I have something for you." She reached deep into her garbage bag, which was still scrunched between her legs. Father Mike noticed straw poking out of the bag as Mary Louise rummaged around and began to pull out old fast-food wrappers, underwear, and all sorts of odds and ends. It all came spilling out of the bag and into Father Mike's clean and neat Honda Civic.

At last Mary Louise stopped digging. She turned and looked Father Mike straight in the eye. Her voice was steady, no longer babbling. She very clearly said: "Michael, this is for you. Use it." From the pile of belongings she produced a brand-new journal, still wrapped in its plastic casing.

"I will," Father Mike said, dumbfounded. "Thank you." Mary Louise instantly reverted to her mumbling and eye-darting. Father Mike opened the door to let Mary Louise out. They embraced, and Mary Louise grabbed her garbage bag, squeezing it in her arms as she headed toward the mall. Father Mike stood beside his car watching Mary Louise walk away, feeling astounded at what had just transpired. He marveled at how God continues to "speak to us in the most unlikely places when we are open to the Holy Spirit." Father Mike expressed that being with Mary Louise was indeed a profound lesson for him. He said, "God is always communicating to us and always taking care of even our smallest needs."

Father Mike believed that "Mary Louise was God handing me the journal himself," and he thanked God for the grace to recognize that Christ was living in Mary Louise, just as he lives in all of us.

This happened many years ago, yet whenever Father Mike considers Blessed Teresa's referral of someone who is in the "distressing disguise of the poorest of the poor," he sees Mary Louise's face in his mind. The lesson he learned by being attentive to Mary Louise — which he recognizes as a formative and essential part of his spirituality — has been confirmed to him over and over again: We are to take care of Jesus in each other.

"Jesus" in Rome

Early in 2008, I attended a three-day international congress at the Vatican to study *Mulieris Dignitatem* (On the Dignity and Vocation of Women). The congress was occasioned by the twentieth anniversary of the apostolic letter, which was written by Blessed John Paul II. It was such a privilege to have been invited by the Holy See, along with 259 other women from around the world. After the amazing congress and audience with Pope Benedict XVI, I visited the beautiful St. Peter's Basilica, the Vatican museum, and many lovely holy places. I was also able to pilgrimage to Assisi with two of my daughters, Chaldea and Mary-Catherine. It was both an exciting and contemplative time.

On one of our days in Rome, we ventured out to some street markets to experience the culture and see the sights. While my oldest daughter, Chaldea, was pursuing the street wares in one location, seventeen-year-old Mary-Catherine and I were headed in another direction. We turned a corner and came upon an elderly woman sitting on the very edge of the street, her crippled legs outstretched with crutches at either side. I felt very distraught to see her sitting flat on the street on pieces of cardboard. I wanted to scoop her up in my arms and move her to a better — and safer — location. I wanted to hold her tight and take away all of her infirmities.

As I approached the woman, tears began to roll down my cheeks. She had what appeared to be tumors all over her head, big knotty bumps poking through her sparse wisps of gray hair. I sensed that Mary-Catherine, who was standing by my side, knew that I was upset about this woman's suffering. She asked me if I had a Miraculous Medal with me to give to her. I knew that I didn't because I didn't bring my purse with me. Eyeing the cup of coins beside her, I reached into my pocket for some money.

Along with the cash, I pulled out a large Miraculous Medal, set on a key chain, that had been blessed by Pope Benedict a couple of days earlier during my audience with him. I kissed it and handed it to her. She kissed it too and mumbled something. She seemed to thank me. She didn't put it into her cup, but gave it an extra squeeze and put it in the pocket of her dress. I told her that it was blessed by the Pope. I didn't know if she could understand my English, but I kept right on talking and pointing toward the Vatican as I explained the blessing from the Pope. I pointed to the image of Mary on the medal and said, "Mary!" The woman nodded as if she understood and spoke in her garbled language. My tears at this point were uncontrollable. I wiped them away, trying not to draw attention to the emotions I felt over seeing this woman sitting on the street in her ragged clothes. It wasn't as if I had never seen a homeless person before, but this particular experience was extraordinary. I was so moved by her.

I asked her if we could say a prayer together. I started to bless myself with the Sign of the Cross, and she did the same. I prayed the Our Father out loud with her, and she seemed to be praying with me, mumbling along. I moved on to the Hail Mary and then again blessed myself with the Sign of the Cross. Mary-Catherine prayed along with us.

I couldn't leave this woman. I had such a hard time seeing her sitting there on the street with her stiff legs straight out in front of her. She looked up into my eyes. Her head had been bent down most of the time. As she looked at me, I took her hands in mine and began kissing her hands. I was overwhelmed, and, in a powerful way, I was filled with such tremendous love for this woman that I actually saw as Jesus in the distressing disguise of the poorest of the poor. My tears continued, and the extraordinary graces prevailed. I put my hands around her face affectionately and kissed her hands again. She wiped her tears away with a tissue. I then traced a cross on her forehead. It took me a very long time before I could part from her because I didn't want to leave her on the street. We said what seemed like a million good-byes. As difficult as it was to leave this woman, I feel that we brought her some love, by God's grace.

My heart was exploding with the love for Jesus, and I felt profoundly moved by his love. That's what Our Lord taught me through Mother Teresa, that simple, humble, loving Albanian nun who came into my life.

March 7, 1988

Dear Donna,

Thankyou very much for your letter
dated January 28, 1988. Being so busy
with our many works for the poor, I
cannot attend to your request. I assure
you of my prayers, but please do contact
a priest near you who may be able to
guide and direct this most beautiful
inspiration to serve Jesus as Apostles
of the Blessed Sacrament.

" I looked for one to comfort me, and
I found none" were the words of Jesus
so through your apostolate of
adoration try to be the "One" to love,
to console, to comfort Jesus.

God bless you
M Teresa

Nine

THE POWER OF LOVE

The power of love was never at rest with Mother Teresa and her sisters, brothers, and priests. One time a man came to Nirmal Hriday (the House of the Dying) in Calcutta. He walked in and — like a man on a mission — went straight over to the women's section of the facility. Amongst the ill and dying women being cared for by the sisters was a woman who had just arrived by ambulance. She was full of worms and covered in dirt. The man very intently observed the sister who was caring for this woman. He looked down at the nun's hands while she was removing the worms; he noticed the loving way she looked at this suffering woman. He looked at the sister's eyes, too.

After some time the man was finished watching. He walked over to Mother Teresa and told her that he had come into the house an angry man, but he was leaving that place a changed one. Observing the love so clearly expressed in the care of the dying there, the man experienced a profound conversion of heart and soul. Faithful love in action is powerful!

Another time, Mother Teresa told the story of a man she picked up off the streets whose body was half-eaten away from worms and maggots. She said that his stench was too much for the others to bear, so she cared for him herself. It took about three hours to remove the worms that were crawling into his flesh and feasting on it, because they had to be extracted one at a time. While she was taking care of the man, he looked at her and asked: "Why are you doing this for me? Everyone else has thrown me away." His eyes told the story of the intense pain he had experienced by being abandoned by everyone — which hurt him more than the attacking worms and disease.

Mother Teresa replied: "I love you; you are Jesus in this distressing disguise. Jesus is sharing his Passion with you." The man said, "But you are sharing that Passion too, right?" Mother Teresa said, "I'm sharing the joy of loving Jesus with you." Then the man (who was a Hindu) said, "Glory be to Jesus Christ!" He never complained about the worms or any discomfort; as Mother Teresa said, "He was just so happy when he realized that he was somebody and that he was loved." The Hindu praised Jesus because of Mother Teresa's loving heart.

Another man whom Mother Teresa retrieved from the streets was also covered with worms. It took quite some time to clean him up. The man said, "I have lived like an animal in the streets, and now I will die like an angel in love and care." After a time of prayer, the man asked to be baptized. Shortly afterward the man told Mother Teresa, "I am going home to God." He then died very peacefully, with a radiant smile on his face.

Mother Teresa's great love hugged the entire globe. She was driven to spread the Gospel message of love to the whole world. She shared her experience of entering Moscow. She told the government that she and her sisters would bring tender love and care to the poor. Mother Teresa and her sisters were allowed to work at a hospital there. Their first job was to clean the toilets, which they humbly accepted with joy. They continued to do all kinds of menial tasks with dedication. They arranged for the local priest to bring in a tabernacle, which they put in a small chapel they set up so that weekly Mass would be available for the people there.

After one week, the doctor came to Mother Teresa and wanted to know what was going on. "Why is everyone more loving; why are the patients more content?" He wanted to know what the sisters were doing that brought about this change of attitude. Mother Teresa replied: "Jesus is in this house now, in the little chapel, loving us all. That's where all the joy, peace, and love are coming from." Amazingly, he thanked her. Mother Teresa deserves a lot of credit for being clever enough to figure out how to get Jesus into Moscow and other places where he was previously unaccepted!

Father Peter Towsley spent time with Mother Teresa and her sisters when Mother Teresa visited her convents in the United States. He told me that he was struck by how "extraordinarily ordinary" Mother Teresa seemed to be. The first time he met her at the contemplative house in the Bronx, he said that people were surrounding her, and his immediate feeling was that she "needed protection" because she appeared to be frail and small. He didn't want her hurt in any way. He vividly remembers speaking with Mother Teresa in the chapel there when she was in a wheelchair because of weakness. Another Missionary of Charity sister stood in the doorway of the chapel,

Mother Teresa coming out of a Mass we both attended at a church in New York.

beckoning Father Peter to come with her, but Mother Teresa had another idea and insisted that Father Peter stay in the chapel to finish their conversation. She looked toward the doorway and, with a sort of admonishing look directed to her fellow sister, got the point across. She undoubtedly felt a vital need to speak with Father Peter at that moment. Who would argue with Mother Teresa?

One by one

This is yet another example of something Mother Teresa taught me about her "one by one" point of view of serving Jesus in others. We treat each person individually, one at a time. Of course, there are times when groups of people are helped, but there are many more times when we minister to one at a time. Each person is unique and important — a child of God.

Mother Teresa obviously had a good reason to continue her conversation with Father Peter in the chapel, and that experience has stayed with Father Peter all these years. I have no doubt that Mother Teresa's words and presence have affected him greatly and that he was also able to pass on these blessings to others in his ministry as a priest and pastor. We all happen upon others in many circumstances throughout our days, even very brief or simple encounters. We may want to take a little time and ponder how we treat each one — how we serve Jesus in them, by allowing Jesus to live through us.

Father Peter shared with me a vivid image that stands out in his mind when he thinks about Mother Teresa's work with the poor. When Blessed John Paul II visited Nirmal Hriday in Calcutta, he asked if he could assist with the care of the dying and was directed to a dying man. The Pontiff attempted to pick up the man in his arms to raise him into a sitting position so he could feed him. Mother Teresa, who was observing from across the room, came over and showed Blessed John Paul II how to position his arms around the man more effectively. The embodiment of the two of them together serving the poorest of the poor was very profound to Father Peter. He said that the marvelous part of this scenario was that they both guided each other — "truth and love together" is how he described it. Father Peter saw "the mutual complementarity of the sexes in the sense of how one needs the other" in this example of the Holy Father and Mother Teresa. "Love without truth would be only sentimentality, and truth without love would be totalitarian; both love and truth need to be guided by each other," he explained.

I can only imagine the beauty, wisdom, and care illustrated in that act of love for the poor administered by Mother Teresa and Blessed John Paul II — a big strong man (before the devastation of his illness got hold of him) being aided by a very small woman to serve the dying man — together allowing Jesus to love through them to serve Jesus in him. Knowing of their great love for each other and their mutual holiness makes the scene especially vivid and beautiful to me.

Life is good

One day my daughter Mary-Catherine and I went with my godmother, Aunt Bertha, and her daughter to visit my uncle who was recovering from a stroke. While talking to Aunt Bertha in my uncle's driveway, I spotted a sticker on the dashboard of her car. "Life is good," it said. I smiled and told my aunt, "Yes, it is!" Aunt Bertha has always been an optimistic person, so to me it was very apropos for her to own this sticker. She immediately peeled off the sticker and handed it to me. "Put it in your car," she told me. So I did, and it became a subtle (or not-so-subtle!) visible reminder to all who traveled in my vehicle with me.

Just a couple of days later, when I was driving home down the country dirt road that led to my house, I saw my neighbor Mona standing by her mailbox. I stopped, and we chatted. She peered into my vehicle and saw my new sticker, bold as can be, as if it could shout, "Life is good!"

She nodded her head slowly and meditatively. "Yes, it is," she said calmly. I peeled it off of my dashboard and handed it to her through my open window so she could display it in her own vehicle. I wanted her to have it, but what was I thinking? How dare I have the audacity to even suggest that "life is good" to a woman whose husband had died tragically only the day before? How could I pretend that life is good, knowing that this woman's husband fell to his untimely death from a tree while he was working hard to provide for his family at his tree removal business?

This woman was suddenly left alone to raise her four young daughters. There was no warning — no time to prepare. Her soul mate and devoted husband had been snatched from her without even the chance to say goodbye. Her head must have been filled with "what ifs," and her heart was surely feeling pummeled. The familiar rhythm of her family's life had changed in that instant forever.

And yet there I was sitting in my vehicle, handing Mona an absurd statement, knowing full well her state of affairs. I knew Mona, though, and had witnessed her strength the day before when my children and I went over to her house in haste to embrace the family upon hearing the news of her husband's tragic death. To say that we were in shock would be an absolute understatement. Mona was standing in the doorway of her house when we approached. She was hugging her sobbing daughters — a pillar of strength for her children. I was utterly amazed to see her standing there. *The power of love,* I thought.

By the mailbox the next day, in the crux of her personal tragedy, this woman shone brilliantly and emanated that life is good. Somehow life was going to be good for them, by God's good grace.

In the book of Corinthians we read, "But he said to me, 'My grace is sufficient for you, for power is made perfect in weakness.' So, I will boast all the more gladly of my weaknesses, so that the power of Christ may dwell in me. Therefore I am content with weaknesses, insults, hardships, persecutions, and calamities for the sake of Christ; for whenever I am weak, then I am strong" (2 Cor 12:9–11).

Blessed John Paul II told us, at an anointing of the sick ceremony: "The sick, the elderly, the handicapped, and the dying teach us that weakness is a creative part of human living, and that suffering can be embraced with no loss of dignity. Without the presence of those people in our midst we might be tempted to think of health, strength, and power as the only important values to be pursued in life. But the wisdom of Christ and the power of Christ are to be seen in the weakness of those who share his sufferings." Just as Blessed John Paul had explained, Mona served as an example of absolute suffering embraced without loss of dignity.

We find courage in Jesus and learn a basic principle of the Christian faith: that there is a mysterious fruitfulness that comes from every sacrifice since the offering of the greatest sacrifice on Calvary. All who suffer are called to unite themselves with Christ's redemptive sacrifice and ask God to transform the suffering into an offering of love and redemption.

Jesus has said, "Very truly, I tell you, unless a grain of wheat falls into the earth and dies, it remains just a single grain; but if it dies, it bears much fruit" (Jn 12:24). When we follow Christ with faith and accept the suffering that comes to us, uniting our pain to Jesus, we are given a precious and mysterious gift of grace. The gift of faith that is ours for the asking helps us to discover the underlying meaning and gift in suffering. With this gift comes an experience of joy that is humanly unexplainable. Christ's promises through the beatitudes nourish our hope. Life is good at every moment, even when it may seem absurd to think so.

A few months after Mona's husband died, I was driving her daughter home after an overnight visit at our house. Fifteen-year-old Allison seemed a little quieter than usual to me. I thought that most likely her silence could be attributed to being overtired from staying up so late the night before, but I ventured to ask. "What are you thinking about, Allison? A penny for your thoughts," I said, hoping to put her at ease.

I received an unexpected and sweet reply: "I was just thinking about how much my father has been helping us lately. My mom wasn't able to get snow tires on the car until this past week, and it was just in time for the snow. And we finally got our new furnace hooked up, and it happened to be right before the freezing weather came."

The power of love in prayer

I met a man at one of my book signings who shared a story with me about his wife's distressing attempt at childbirth. She was due to have her baby when serious and totally unexpected complications suddenly arose. The doctor had instructed her to go to the hospital, and when she arrived the use of a fetal monitor revealed that the baby's heartbeat was slowing down. The doctor attached a fetal heart monitor to the baby's head to track the level of distress, and he put the woman on a labor-inducing intravenous drip. The doctor wanted to hasten the labor to get the baby safely delivered. In his hurry though, he gave this mother too much of the labor-inducing drug.

Suddenly, the expectant mother's vital signs became dangerously pronounced. She went into immediate, life-threatening distress. Her uterus ruptured, causing the baby to partially escape from the uterus into the mother's body. The mother was severely hemorrhaging, and attempts to save the mother and baby's life through surgery began immediately.

The outcome did not look very promising at all. Family members were contacted immediately by phone. Word quickly also spread to members of the parish about their need for immediate and intense prayer, which produced an instantaneous onslaught of prayers beseeching heaven.

One parishioner, Patricia, whom I also met at the book signing that day, told me that she cried out to God, almost feeling mad at him, "Why are you taking them both?" Everyone prayed at home, at Mass, and before the Blessed Sacrament, pleading for help for their beloved friend and her unborn baby. The outpouring of love and prayers from this mother's parish community played a powerful role in a very happy ending for this family. The mother came through the high-risk surgery exceptionally well, and little baby Eleanor was born safely. Thanks be to God!

A few weeks later, the family was able to attend Mass together at their parish. When they walked in, a hush came over the congregation as they turned to see the family carrying their little swaddled Eleanor. To see this mom and baby come into the church when a few weeks earlier both of their lives had been in jeopardy was a sight to behold and a reassurance to everyone about the power of love and prayer.

A life-transforming gesture

There are many, many instances of the power of love through prayer. My dear friend Father Bill Smith shared a beautiful story with me to illustrate how a soul in love with God worked a miracle in a stranger's heart.

One morning after Mass, Father Bill went to get the Blessed Sacrament to bring to the sick in a nursing home. He went into a quiet church and genuflected reverently before the tabernacle. He proceeded to put the necessary amount of consecrated Hosts into his pyx and genuflected again upon closing the tabernacle door. He then headed out to the nursing home.

It turns out that during the same time, a man had entered the church out of curiosity. He wanted to look around when no one else was there. When he saw Father Bill, the man quickly hid behind the curtain in the confessional, where he was still able to observe the priest retrieving the Blessed Sacrament from the tabernacle.

The man hiding in the confessional experienced a profound conversion. He witnessed the love this priest had for Jesus in the Blessed Sacrament as he observed the priest bowing down reverently, exuding love for his Eucharistic Lord.

The following day, the man returned to the church, but this time he went to the rectory to find the priest. When Father Bill answered the door, the man told him the whole story, explaining how he had been hiding in the church the day before. He then expressed a deep desire to become a Catholic so that he could experience this same love for Jesus that was so apparent to him when observing the priest. An act of love for Jesus by this priest and the grace of God brought this man to his knees, literally, and into the Church — such is the power of love!

No matter where we find ourselves in life — homemakers reaching out to our neighbors, priests or religious serving the needy here in the United States or in some Third World country, members of the Church praying for each other in times of crisis — we can all serve Jesus as Mother Teresa did.

Dear Donna

I thank you for your beautiful letter .
Thank you for all you are to Jesus
through the 'Lay Missionaries of Charity'.
I am sure, that for you is the surest way
of satiating the thirst of Jesus on the
Cross for love of one another in your
own family.

Fidelity to growing into a soul of prayer
is the beginning of great holiness. If
we remember 'what we do to Jesus — that we
do to each other', we would be real
contemplatives in the heart of the world.
Let us learn to pray and work as Jesus
did for 30 years in Nazareth. The life and
work; the prayer and sacrifice at Nazareth
are so much like what our life should be.
That peace, joy and unity that joined the
Holy Family together in prayer and work
is such a wonderful living example to us.
They grew in holiness together. Let us
learn from Mary to pray and ask Her to
pray that your home will be another Nazareth

God bless you
Lee Teresa mc

Ten

GOD LOVES SILENCE

We are surrounded by noise. We live in a world of distraction. With so much overstimulation, it is difficult to settle down and find any peace and quiet, within or without. Sometimes even our own thoughts can prevent us from being quiet in our souls. When there is a momentary pause, we quickly fill it with something. We think about yesterday, we worry about tomorrow, and we have great difficulty staying in the present moments of our lives.

People today seem to crave noise as well as more and more activity. Some of us cannot travel without headphones or a Bluetooth on our ears, listening to music or carrying on phone conversations constantly. Our technological world has made the search for silence much more complex.

Are we afraid of our own thoughts? Do we have such a need to distract ourselves with activity and racket that we miss the graces that Our Lord wishes to bestow on us through silence? Do we unconsciously tune him out? Why is it that when that rare opportunity for quiet presents itself we fill the void with something, rather than sit still and embrace the silence?

Unless we are living in a monastery or convent, it's difficult to encounter silence on a regular basis. Even if we don't choose to smother ourselves with constant noise, there are others around us who do, and this overlaps our space, intruding on our preference to be independent and liberated from noise. I have even found this to be true in church. I've observed those at church who seem oblivious to the fact that Mass is in progress, and they find it necessary to speak to one another about insignificant trivial things, sometimes rather loudly. It would seem as though nothing is sacred anymore.

"We need silence to be able to touch souls," Blessed Teresa said. Her deep union with God taught her the silence of the heart. Living the life of the poor in Calcutta, she voluntarily took on the spirit and reality of poverty and ministered to the poorest of the poor on the dirty streets of Calcutta. How does one find silence in such a noisy city, we wonder.

Blessed Teresa has also said: "The first requirement for prayer is silence. Silence will teach us a lot. It will teach us to speak with Christ and to speak joyfully to our brothers and sisters." Mother Teresa taught her Missionaries of Charity sisters the necessity of seeking the silence of the heart in order to reach God. She told them that without God and a deep prayer life they would only be social workers. She instructed her sisters to spend time in silence with Jesus in the Blessed Sacrament each day and to listen to God during their time with him to know his will for them individually. She encouraged them to continuously seek Jesus in their quieted hearts so that they would be able to allow Jesus to dwell within them, radiating his love out to all they met.

Within silence, a world of wisdom, grace, and truth unfolds, saturating the heart. These gifts are available to all who search for them with a pure heart. A deeper union with God is obtainable once we empty our hearts of all that stands in the way of our pursuit of him.

Jesus spent thirty of his thirty-three years on earth in silence during his quiet life with his mother, Mary, and Joseph, his foster father. He began his first forty days of public life in silence. We know from the Gospels that Jesus often retreated to silence in the mountains or the desert, immersing himself in deep prayer, particularly at intense times.

There were many instances when Jesus chose to be silent rather than to speak. Blessed Teresa calls attention to Jesus' silence: "Let us admire Christ's compassion toward Judas. The Master kept a holy silence: He did not want to reveal his betrayer in front of his comrades. Jesus could have easily spoken out and unveiled the hidden intentions of Judas. He preferred mercy rather than condemnation. He called him friend. If Judas had looked in Jesus' eyes, he would surely have been the friend of God's mercy."

Come to the quiet

We can learn an example of quieting the mind and soul from the Psalms: "I do not occupy myself with things too great and too marvelous for me. But I have calmed and quieted my soul, like a weaned child with its mother" (Ps 131:1–2).

Blessed Teresa advises us to learn from St. Augustine, who said, "Fill yourselves first and then only will you be able to give to others." Blessed Teresa instructs us that, if we really want God to fill us, "we must empty ourselves through humility of all that is selfishness in us." In order to be filled with the things of God, we need to empty ourselves of all that gets in the way. He is ready to fill us up. Once we have emptied ourselves, we will begin to listen intently and openly to his whispers in our souls. Mother Teresa wisely taught, recounted in *Mother Teresa: A Simple Path* (Ballantine Books, 1995):

> *I always begin my prayer in silence, for it is in the silence of the heart that God speaks. We need to listen to God because it's not what we say but what he says to us and through us that matters.*

Each day, the Missionaries of Charity (sisters, brothers, and priests) start with prayer, and then participation at holy Mass in humble, simple chapels with bare floors, lacking kneelers, pews, chairs, or ornamentation — only ambitious, thirsting hearts desiring to come closer to God. Don't forget — those two simple yet poignant words, "I thirst," mark all of their convent's chapels throughout the world, representing Jesus' thirst for souls and serving as a reminder of his insatiable desire and thirst for our love. The simplicity of the Missionaries of Charity's lives draws them to silence, where a deeper meaningful prayer life, an opening up to the fullness of the Truth, is fulfilled in their hearts.

Blessed Teresa of Calcutta learned early on when she founded the Missionaries of Charity that in order to properly care for the poor, time in silence before Jesus in the Blessed Sacrament was absolutely necessary. And so, in addition to their morning prayers, prayers throughout the day, prayers at holy Mass, and evening prayers, they spend at least an hour in silence with Jesus in prayer before the Blessed Sacrament, where he waits in the tabernacle. As Mother Teresa said: "Jesus always waits for us in silence. In silence he listens to us; in silence he speaks to our souls. In silence we are granted the privilege of listening to his voice."

Inner silence does not necessarily come easily. It requires a real effort and desire to actually find it and cultivate it. When we quiet ourselves long enough to seek Our Lord in silence, we will discover a new vision, renewed energy, and a real unity with Our Lord.

I was very fortunate to have experienced the spirit of silence in the Missionaries of Charity convents and chapels at various locations. One time, when I visited the sisters at their convent in the Bronx, New York, I walked into their quiet chapel at a rare time when it was empty, and I knelt by myself before Our Lord in the Blessed Sacrament. Just a few minutes later, Mother Teresa happened to come into the chapel and knelt quietly on the bare floor nearby, clasping her hands in prayer, bowing her head deeply, and seeking a time for her own silent moments with Jesus. We were both blessed by Jesus during that time together in silence. Wow!

Often we are not able to find Jesus or hear him in all the noise, restlessness, and agitation around us. He is there but difficult for us to recognize. We must take the time to listen to him in silence whenever we can. We need to pause for a while and still ourselves, even if this is not an easy task amid a hectic pace within our ever-busier schedules. However, it will be during those moments of seeking that we will come to realize that God is a friend of silence, and only within silence will we learn the deepest truths.

Blessed Teresa explained how the gift of silence affects the Missionaries of Charity's work with the dying. In washing their wounds, their faces, and their bodies, the sisters shower a pure love upon the poor, all the while praying for them and seeing Jesus within them. Mother Teresa said: "We want these poor to realize that there are people who really love them. Here they find again their human dignity, and they die in an impressive silence. God loves silence."

Mother Teresa gave us another clue to achieving silence of the heart: "Mary will teach us silence, how to keep all things in our hearts as she did, to pray in the silence of our hearts." We can apply this principle of silence to our own lives, asking the Blessed Mother to guide us to her Son in the stillness of our hearts. She will show us the way to him through our silent persevering prayer, giving us much to ponder in our own hearts.

The search for silence

Even amid our crazy lives, we can discover silence. We should certainly search for silence, even when we are busy with our daily tasks. We can train ourselves to be silent in the depths of our souls. When we ask Our Lord to teach us to pray more fervently and more wholeheartedly, he will show us the way to enter the inner oratory of our hearts where we can go to pray often. We can train ourselves to seek silence deep within our hearts.

A mother can find silence even within the noise of her household — in the busyness of caring for her children, folding laundry, cooking a meal, or washing dishes — when she looks inward and offers her heart to God. I am not suggesting that she become oblivious to what she is doing, especially when caring for children. This is a different kind of silence. While folding a load of laundry, cooking her family's dinner, or nursing a baby, a mother can become meditative, raising her heart to God and thanking him for the privilege of serving him as she serves her family within her vocation of motherhood.

A father can discover silence during his everyday tasks at work or at home by asking God to help him find opportune moments to quiet his thoughts briefly and reflect. Even as he is performing a task, he can turn his thoughts and heart to the Lord, if only for a moment, asking for grace, strength, and guidance to continue his work while uniting himself with the Lord.

A student can pause between assignments to retreat to the heart, discreetly praying to God. Those in the workplace can seek silence of the heart throughout their days no matter what they are doing. A moment here and there for prayer during our activities can help us transcend the noise and reveal the inner layer of stillness and silence. Time before Jesus in the Blessed Sacrament, whenever we are able, brings us into silence before God.

Within silence, we find God and we listen to him. St. John of the Cross wrote, "The language God best hears is silent love" *(Maxims and Counsels,* 53). Ironically, silence can be found wherever we are. We have to search for it, though, and listen for it. We say, "Lord, I am yours; do with me what you will." Our hearts pray silently to the Lord. Silence is the key to a more intimate union with God and bears the secret to peace of heart.

Mother Teresa preached a simple path to peace that begins with silence when she said: "The fruit of silence is prayer. The fruit of prayer is faith. The fruit of faith is love. The fruit of love is service. The fruit of service is peace." It all begins with silence.

Try not to concern yourself with frivolous matters or clutter your mind with senseless details. Instead, still your soul and be attentive to your Lord no matter what you are doing. Choose to retreat into your heart and allow God to speak to you in silence whenever you are able.

†
LDM

Missionaries of Charity
54A, Lower Circular Road,
Calcutta- 16 W.B.

14th Sept. 1990.

Dear Donna,

Thank you for your letter of 29.8.1990
with prayers and wishes on the occasion
of my birthday. God bless you for your
thoughtfulness.

I am very glad that you are using the
gift God gave you to spread His love and
mercy to all. Yes, your first apostolate
should be your family - husband and children.

Yes, I will be very glad to receive more
Miraculous medals, rosaries and whatever you
can send for the spiritual apostolate. I
am sure God is very pleased with the wonderful
work you are doing as a Marian Catechist.

Right now I cannot think of opening a new
house in Dankbury CT. But pray much that
later we may be able to send some Sisters.

I will surely remember you specially your
Sister Barbara in my prayers. Tell her that
I assure her of my prayers for her and her
husband.

God loves you - love others as God loves you.

God bless you.

Mc Teresa mc

Eleven

LESSONS IN SIMPLICITY

I have a little sign in my home office that just says, "Simplify." This is what I strive to do — simplify my life to the extent that I am able so I can truly serve the Lord without getting caught up in the clutter of the household and the world. When we de-clutter we feel better; we are more focused and more organized. This is not only a good practice for life in general, but an aid in our spiritual lives as well.

Blessed Teresa stayed very simple: simple in her dress, choosing only a cotton sari rather than a silk one; simple in her preaching; and, most importantly, simple in her relationship with God. She sought him completely and wholeheartedly, never permitting anything to get in the way of her union with him.

The definition of simplicity is a lack of complexity, embellishment, difficulty, and complication. Where do we find simplicity in our convoluted world? Should we seek to live a less complicated life? Aren't we encouraged to discover whatever is out there — to make use of the latest modern technology?

Let's consider the Holy Family of Nazareth. Although set deeply in the past, we can draw wisdom from the Holy Family's decision to remain simple, humble, and uncomplicated. Being forced to give birth in an animal's home because there was no room at the inn was not the only reason Mary and Joseph found themselves in a cold stable in the midst of flies, animals, and manure. Also in their midst was the humility, obedience, simplicity, holiness, and silence that enveloped the Holy Family in Bethlehem.

It's so interesting that heaven's glory was manifested in poverty. Our Savior's birth took place very quietly, hardly what one would expect for a king's birth — a holy occurrence of extreme magnitude. Jesus, who was certainly entitled to a royal and pampered birth, was not born in a palace, but instead rested his sacred head on a bed of straw in a simple manger. Common shepherds were the first witnesses to the awesome event of the birth of the Messiah.

In our own day, what is the value of being simple? How can we embrace simplicity when our culture advances us forward with consumerism, technology, and science? If we merely go along with what the world dictates, we might be dragged down to hell. We should be aware that our culture is not necessarily directing us forward, but instead in another direction, an approach we would rather not move toward.

The Holy Spirit can help us to become simple and trusting in God alone, knowing that he is all good, loving, and merciful. We can simplify our lives and remain uncomplicated by praying for the graces to follow God's will for us. We can ask Our Lord each day to use us as he wills. If we offer our hearts unreservedly to him, we can be assured without a doubt that we will possess a deep peace, no matter what is happening around us. We will become aware that coincidences don't exist and that God is in control.

My two o'clock appointment

Amazing things can happen in seemingly simple ways. My friend Sister Mary Frances has a favorite saying: "Every disappointment is God's appointment!" She never worries about a thing because she knows that God is always in control. I've had my own experiences that bear this out. I believe that sometimes God allows us glimpses of his work, and at other times we simply trust that he knows what's best when appointments get rearranged or things don't turn out as we had planned.

I had scheduled an appointment with my parish priest and looked forward to spending some time with him. The day of the appointment arrived, and as two o'clock approached, I went over to the parish center to meet with Father Tom. Upon arriving, I was told by Chris, the parish secretary, that Father Tom had called to say that he was at the hospital with Father Mike, who had hurt his arm at the children's picnic during a game of tug of war."She told me she wasn't able to reach me in time by phone to tell me about the change of events. Father Tom apologized and asked Chris to let me know that he would reschedule our meeting for another time.

She quickly brought to my attention the fact that there was a woman waiting in the next room who had come to her own two o'clock appointment. Her meeting was with Father Mike, the one who was injured. Chris was feeling at a loss because the woman had become visibly upset upon hearing of Father Mike's absence. When Chris had finished whispering this to me, the woman poked her head around the doorway to see who had just arrived.

"Ave Maria!" I exclaimed. (Believe it or not, that was actually her name.) "How are you? How are you feeling?" I asked her.

She had endured quite a bit of suffering because of a very bad car accident she'd recently been in while in Florida. She was a passenger in the car and was on her way to visit her brother, who was in the hospital at the time. Ave Maria ended up spending the next month in the intensive care unit of another Florida hospital. She was back home in Connecticut and slowly recovering, but she was dealing with neurological and pain issues.

The secretary quickly chimed in before Ave Maria could even respond to my greeting. "Donna, do you have a little time? Would you be able to meet with Ave Maria? I think she would love to talk with you."

One look at Chris' troubled face made it obvious that she was pleading for my help. She had heard the panic in Ave Maria's voice and witnessed her anguish. She had already tried her best to console this woman, but to no avail. I certainly had time. I had reserved this time for my two o'clock appointment, and interestingly enough, my "two o'clock appointment" was at the hospital taking care of Father Mike, Ave Maria's "two o'clock appointment."

"Of course," I replied.

Ave Maria thanked me, and we went off to a quiet room. We sat across from each other, and Ave Maria explained her most recent feelings of despair to me. She felt deeply troubled by them.

"I just don't know what to do," she said sadly. "God just doesn't hear me anymore; I just can't feel a thing. My prayers are worthless. I'm ready to give up, and that's why I was here to see Father Mike." Her eyes were filling with tears.

"Oh, Ave Maria, your prayers are not worthless at all!" The words just poured out. "God loves you very much," I said. "Sometimes it feels like your prayers aren't heard, but don't worry about how you feel. You are a faithful, prayerful woman. Right now, you are experiencing a 'dark night of the soul.' You have been through so much. I am convinced that Jesus loves you so much that he actually has allowed you to come so close to him on the cross that he can kiss you!"

I was sharing some of the same words Mother Teresa had used to console me when I was undergoing a huge trial. I told Ave Maria about Mother Teresa's own personal dark night of the soul that was made known after her death. Mother Teresa kept what she called "the darkness" hidden from the world, and even from those closest to her. Her pain was deep and devastating. She longed for Jesus' love, but she had to endure the feelings of being rejected and separated by God. Mother Teresa's darkness began around the time she started her work with the poor and continued to the end of her life, as she mystically participated in the thirst of Jesus along with him.

I could tell that these words comforted Ave Maria, because as I spoke to her I witnessed a remarkable transformation. She visibly calmed down. She exhaled deeply, actually blowing air out of her pursed lips. Her shoulders relaxed and came down, and her facial expression softened. She sighed deeply several times. I reached out and took her hands in mine, and she shed some tears talking about her accident, her brother's sickness and subsequent death, her lengthy stay at the hospital, her fears, her pain, and even some serious family issues that she faced when she came back home.

If that was not enough, the worst pain for her came after all of that, I think. She was feeling as though the God she loved so dearly had deserted her, because she could no longer feel his love at all. Everything seemed bleak, dark, and hopeless to her. But now the darkness was giving way to a peaceful, calming light as we spoke. She felt the strength to trust Our Lord again.

It's truly awe-inspiring when we see and experience glimpses of God at work. That's what I saw at that two o'clock appointment. God had his plan for Ave Maria, Father Mike, Father Tom, and me. He had it all under control, and I was happy to be his instrument. The secretary told me later that she was at her wit's end, not knowing whom she should call to help this distraught woman. That's when I walked in, by the grace of God's timing.

Ave Maria and I sat and talked for a while longer. I suggested that she tell her doctor about the hopeless feelings she had been experiencing, but to certainly take it all to the Divine Physician as well. I advised her to visit Jesus in the Blessed Sacrament often, where she could pour out her heart to him and experience his peace. I gave her a Miraculous Medal that had touched the one Mother Teresa gave me. When we parted, she left the room with tremendous hope in her heart and a smile on her face. God is good!

I stopped by our church directly afterward to meet Jesus in the Blessed Sacrament. I had invited Ave Maria to come with me, but she needed to pick up her grandson and couldn't be late. The church was quiet, and I walked in and knelt down before the tabernacle, thanking God for his great love and the special graces we had just experienced. The rectory was right next door to the church, so when I was finished praying I decided to stop and see if the two priests were back from the hospital.

Father Mike answered the door with his arm in a sling. After expressing concern about his injury, I filled him in on what had just transpired.

"I took your two o'clock appointment," I said with a smile.

"I don't quite understand," he said with a puzzled look.

"Ave Maria," I said. "She was there waiting for you, and she was very upset, so I met with her temporarily until you can see her," I explained.

A smile spread across his face as he began to comprehend the scenario. He thanked me and assured me that he had already planned to call her and that he appreciated being told about the urgency of the matter.

A few months later, Ave Maria was sitting at her sister Nancy's deathbed. Nancy had worked with the Missionaries of Charity in Bombay. But now she lay quietly, her body ravaged by cancer, preparing to meet her Lord. Ave Maria pulled out the Miraculous Medal that I had given her and used it to bless her sister before she died.

Encounters at the shopping mall

At one of my book signings at the largest shopping mall in the Northeast, I sat at a big table situated right near the bookstore's doorway, facing the main corridor of the mall — a very visible location. My books were displayed on the table along with a small sign and a couple of pens. I placed a small picture of Mother Teresa in front of my books. I sat there at my post and smiled and greeted the people walking by.

Many people stopped by to chat and to have me sign copies of my books. Mother Teresa's picture drew attention and sparked lots of heartwarming conversation; so many people love and revere her. One couple ambled by, pushing their sleeping child in a stroller. The father was a fairly large, muscular man with many tattoos decorating his arms. He looked like a tough guy — tough enough to withstand getting all those tattoos! — but looks can be deceiving. The mother was quietly walking beside him. The father stopped in front of me when he saw Mother Teresa's picture. His heart seemed to melt right there, and he expressed a deep love for Mother Teresa. He also told me that he was a Catholic.

As we chatted, his wife was very quiet and their toddler slept away in the stroller. I gave them each a prayer card of Mother Teresa and blessed Miraculous Medals for the three of them. (I decided a while back to carry on a tradition of Mother Teresa's by giving out Miraculous Medals to everyone I meet at book signings and events.) This family accepted my little gifts, shook my hand, and walked away seemingly happy and content.

Within a few moments, the father came back and said, "My wife is over there," he pointed, then paused and composed himself. "She's crying," he continued, visibly moved, and then he took another breath. "She wants your book," he said, "and she's Jewish!" I signed one of my books for her, and as he purchased it, he explained that his wife was so moved after talking with me and receiving the prayer card and the Miraculous Medal that she just had to have the book even though the first word in the title was "Catholic."

These types of encounters are very touching to my heart. I am always amazed at how God works and am truly thankful that he can use a simple instrument to bring others closer to him. It is my heart's desire to allow him to love through me.

At another book signing the following year at that same store, a woman walking past stopped to talk with me. Even though she didn't appear to be interested in my books, she was eager to tell me about herself. She confessed that she had left the Church years ago and was "searching." I listened and looked into her eyes as she poured out her story to me.

Mother Teresa, processing down the aisle, looks at my daughter Chaldea, who handed her a note and a picture (Washington, DC, cathedral).

As I responded to her, I saw that a tear had formed in the corner of her eye. I felt moved to take her hand in mine as we talked. The tiny tear in her eye became floods of tears that kept pouring down her face and onto my table. Then the woman's face seemed to transform before my eyes, and she said, "Please sign a book for me. I have to read it." I signed a book and stood up to embrace her. She left, expressing her gratitude and wiping her tears, appearing happy and peaceful. I have continued to pray for this woman.

There really are no coincidences in life! I truly believe that when we ask Our Lord to use us, amazing things will take place. It starts every morning when we open our eyes and ask Our Lord to use us this day to spread his love and to do his will.

Simple words, simple actions

It's amazing how a simple word or gesture can help to convert someone's heart, by God's grace. We can never imagine the effect our words might have on someone; God might very well be working in their hearts, and our providential conversation might be just the trigger to respond to his love, often with tears.

We are a people who are broken and in need of healing. Our Lord comes to us in love, wanting to heal our brokenness. He also wants to use us to minister to others. As we give him our hearts and lives unreservedly, he will work through us to touch others. Blessed Teresa expressed it this way:

Jesus comes to meet us. To welcome him, let us go to meet him. He comes to us in the hungry, the naked, the lonely, the alcoholic, the drug addict, the prostitute, the street beggar. He may come to you or me in a father who is alone, in a mother, in a brother, or in a sister. If we reject them, if we do not go out to meet them, we reject Jesus himself. (Mother Teresa: In My Own Words, Gramercy, 1996)

Make it your goal to meet Jesus in everyone that God in his goodness surrounds you with. You can be sure that a greater meaning and mission is hidden below the surface of what meets the eye. If you allow the love of Christ to guide you, you'll never go wrong, and miracles will happen, born out of grace, trust, and simplicity.

MISSIONARIES OF CHARITY
54A A.J.C. BOSE ROAD
CALCUTTA — 700016

Sept 2, ' 91

Dear Donna,

I have just recently returned after
some months absence and so could
not reply your letter earlier. Thank
you for writing and for also sending
a copy of the book you are writing.

Do not be afraid. Just put yourself
in the Hands of our Blessed Mother
and let her take care of you. When
you are afraid or sad or troubled
just tell her so. She will prove
Herself a Mother to you. Pray often:
" Mary, Mother of Jesus, make me
alright"; " Mary, Mother of Jesus,
be Mother to me now." Enclosed is a
miraculous medal. She has done
wonders for others and she will do
so for you too. Just trust and pray
I am praying for you and the baby.

God bless you
lee Teresa me

Twelve

CALCUTTA ALL OVER THE WORLD

Mother Teresa told me, "There is Calcutta all over the world for those who have eyes to see." It is up to us to look for the poor and care for them. The Nobel Prize that Blessed Teresa received not only acknowledged her work with the poor but also awakened consciences in favor of the poor worldwide. She opened our eyes to the fact that the poor are our brothers and sisters, and we have the duty to treat them with love.

It is very possible that you will find human beings, surely very near you, needing affection and love. Do not deny them these. Show them, above all, that you sincerely recognize that they are human beings, that they are important to you. Who is that someone? That person is Jesus himself: Jesus who is hidden under the guise of suffering! (Mother Teresa: In My Own Words, Gramercy, 1996)

She accepted the award in the name of the poor, giving all the credit to God, and she helped raise a deeper awareness of the existence of the poor in our midst. She also reminded us that the poor are not only those who are hungry for a piece of bread. The poor can be someone who is well-off financially, but whose heart is starving for love.

It is hard for me to believe, but there are people who have criticized Blessed Teresa for the way she cared for the poor. She knew that she wasn't called to analyze systems, economic patterns, or ideologies. She simply recognized that every person has a conscience and is called by God to love one another. She was clear that she was called to serve the poor.

Although for the most part Blessed Teresa was well received, respected, and loved, many times she was told that she should not give fish to the poor, but instead provide them with rods so they could learn to fish for themselves. To this she answered: "So often they do not have the strength to hold the rod. Giving them the fish, I help them to recover the strength necessary for the fishing of tomorrow." I admire her tenacity and the fact that she never flinched or cowered in expressing what she felt was necessary.

When asked why she didn't try to fight for justice and human rights or to change structures, she explained that, while she and the Missionaries of Charity were not unaware of those things, "Our mission is to look at the problem more individually and not collectively. We care for a person and not a multitude. We seek the person with whom Jesus Christ identified himself when he said, 'I was hungry, I was sick.'" This was her approach with everyone and everything in which she came in contact. Her simple, trustful outlook may have come up against some criticism, but it never failed.

She summed up the way she cared for the poor by saying: "To know the problem of poverty intellectually is not to understand it. It is not by reading, taking a walk in the slums, admiring, and regretting that we come to understand it and discover what it has of bad and good. We have to dive into it, live it, share it." And this is exactly what she did.

In our own neighborhoods

If there's just one thing I hope to get across in this book, it's that we don't need to rush off to Calcutta to find the poor. The poor undeniably exist in our own backyards and possibly within our own homes. Mother Teresa invites us to look around us very carefully and discern whether there may be a need for us to act. The poor come in many sizes, shapes, colors, and backgrounds. Just because a person appears to be doing well outwardly does not necessarily mean that he or she is doing well interiorly. That's where we come in. Like Mother Teresa, we too need to arm ourselves with deep prayer, humility, and a giving love.

Meeting the poor face-to-face isn't always going to be as dramatic as finding a crippled elderly woman with a head full of tumors sitting on the street. We may discover the poor in the co-worker sitting in the cubicle next to us who wants to share his story. It may be our spouse who longs for more time to be with us, or it could be the woman who lives next door who hides behind her cocktails because she is so hurt that her own daughters won't visit her.

We are all called to love our neighbor, even those who irritate and annoy us, those who steal our parking spaces, those who make fun of our devotion, those who ridicule us, those who belittle us, attack us, and antagonize us — these are the very people we must love and pray for. Maybe they are cranky and unhappy because they are starved for love. A smile, a gesture, or a kind word can work miracles. God puts difficult individuals in our lives for a reason. We may never see the happy outcome, but we must trust, love, and pray, and let God do the work.

Why should we go out of our way to love the people who are unloving to us? Because Jesus asks us to. Isn't that enough? Love can change hearts, and yet real loving often hurts. Jesus sweated blood when he prayed in the Garden of Gethsemane because he loved so intensely. God, in his infinite wisdom, has placed us wherever we find ourselves. It's no coincidence that we may live near an ogre or with a family member who is having difficulties and not acting lovingly toward us. We may have a business colleague who challenges our Christianity constantly. There may be those in our lives who have hurt us unjustly. Blessed Teresa again and again referred to these people as "Jesus in the distressing disguise of the poorest of the poor." These are the people whom God has put in our midst. These are the ones we are called to love, those we are to feed with fish. They may need to be fed on more than one occasion. Then one day, because they were shown love by God's grace through us, they may be strong enough to carry their own rods and feed others.

Additionally, we can seek out those more obviously in need: We could help out at a homeless shelter or soup kitchen, visit those in prison or nursing homes, or help unwed mothers. The list is endless. We are called to roll up our sleeves and give until it hurts, as Mother Teresa so often taught.

All the while, let's keep a joyful spirit. We are human, and we can get cranky. But if we give up grumbling and complaining when we are tired or not feeling inclined to give of ourselves, we will reach more people so much more effectively. Remember, Mother Teresa always stressed that real giving is when it hurts. Along with that sometimes painful giving, remember that "joy is a net to catch souls." She believed that joyful giving is what attracts others to Christianity. She even told her sisters that if they didn't have joy in their hearts, they could pack up and go home. Yes, that's right — go home!

Two altar boys

I heard a true story about two altar boys from opposite sides of the world. The first altar boy, while assisting at a Mass, dropped a cruet of water in a cathedral where the local bishop was celebrating Mass. Needless to say, it caused a disturbance, and the boy was very embarrassed. After Mass, the bishop proceeded to scold the boy profusely for the accident.

On the other side of the world, another altar boy dropped a cruet of wine on the tiled floor of a cathedral while the archbishop was celebrating Mass. Of course, this too created a huge noise and embarrassed the boy. After Mass, the archbishop called the boy into his office and asked him what he wanted to be when he grew up. The boy told the archbishop that he wanted to go to a particular school. The archbishop questioned him further, and then he told the boy he felt he would grow up to be a priest and then an archbishop, just like him. That archbishop's prediction proved to be prophetically correct. The boy did grow up to be a priest and eventually became Archbishop Fulton Sheen.

The boy on the other side of the world was Joseph Stalin, leader of the Communist Party. Can we not help but wonder what would have happened to Stalin had he been treated more lovingly as a youngster? This may seem like a stretch, but I think it's something to think about. Shouldn't we consider our responses and actions at all times, knowing that we influence others for better or for worse?

Transforming grace

Just before my trip to participate at a Vatican congress, my daughter Mary-Catherine and I were on our way home from doing some errands when suddenly I felt as if someone had clobbered me on the back of my head with a baseball bat. That's really the only way I can explain it. It was a sudden and excruciating pain that totally shocked me. I looked over at Mary-Catherine in the passenger seat, and when I saw the bewildered and painful look on her face I knew she had experienced the same thing.

It took us a few seconds to realize that we had been hit from behind. We had been stopped at a crosswalk to allow a pedestrian to cross the street. A big truck came barreling down the road behind us and didn't stop. The driver plowed right through the back of our car. I asked the pedestrian to call 911. My daughter and I were put on body boards and into neck braces, and then transported by ambulance to the emergency room. The very worst part for me was that I couldn't help my daughter. It was the first time in more than thirty-two years when I was physically unable to help one of my children when they needed me. We both had to remain completely still and allow the paramedics to assist us. We did manage to grab each other's hands before we were separated, and we were able to say a few prayers together.

In the emergency room, we waited in separate rooms for x-rays to be taken. As I waited, a woman came into my room and stood at the side of my bed. I could see that someone was standing behind her. She apologized for her son who had crashed into us. I told her that it was okay, and then her son came forward from behind his mother and apologized himself. I told him it was okay, and I then did something that surprised me. I asked him if I could hold his hand. He switched his Dunkin' Donuts coffee cup to his other hand, and with a surprised expression, he took my hand. I couldn't turn my head to directly face him, but I squeezed his hand in mine and said: "It's okay, but you need to pray for my daughter and me. We don't know what's going on with our necks and backs. You need to pray."

Here I was, practically demanding that this seventeen-year-old boy pray for us. I had no idea what his religion was, if any. All I knew was that I felt the Lord speaking through me; I was bold and loving, by God's grace. He had tears in his eyes, and tears streamed down my face too. It was a very emotional time. He said, "I will!" And then I added, "And you need to SLOW DOWN!"

And quietly I also added, "You may never have forgiven yourself if you had killed someone." I really felt the Lord working on that young man right at that moment; I had no doubt in my mind. Before his mother left the room, she thanked me. I told her I was sorry that I spoke to her son that way. She replied: "No, he needed to hear that, he really did! Thank you!"

The next day as I was lying on my loveseat, racked with pain, while Mary-Catherine was nearby on the couch, I thought about the whole ordeal. We had only a week and a half before we embarked on our journey to the Vatican, and now we were in sorry shape. But what had transpired?

Mother Teresa talking to a crowd gathered outside a New York City church after a Mass.

I'm convinced that, because that young man hit our vehicle, we had prevented the pedestrian from being killed or injured by his truck. Contrary to what might seem logical, we were in the right place at the right time. I also feel that God worked another miracle, and that is that someone told that boy to pray. Who knows what was going on in his life at that time? One thing was clear — he needed to focus on his driving and slow down. God gave him someone in the flesh to tell him — not only about his driving, but just as importantly to ask him to pray! Mother Teresa would surely have recognized "Jesus in the distressing disguise" in this young man. She also felt that we're all in too much of a rush. We need to slow down.

We did make it to the Vatican on time. I wore a neck brace during our stay in Rome, and both my daughter and I went through more than a year of physical therapy afterward because of whiplash, brain injuries, and spine issues. We're still not healed totally, but we are very thankful it wasn't worse.

More transformation

I had another experience when I felt Our Lord working to bring transformation out of suffering. The following year, I had a series of severe urinary tract infections. A couple of weeks before Holy Week, my doctor called one evening to tell me that he found a new bacteria in the most recent culture. He told me that I needed to see an infectious disease doctor immediately and receive intravenous infusions. The infection he identified was life-threatening, but hopefully caught early enough. The treatment for this infection was antibiotics, and amputation if needed! If the bacteria gets into the bloodstream, it can be deadly. I had just heard of this sort of infection about a month earlier in the news. A Brazilian model had contracted the same bacteria. Her hands and feet had to be amputated in an attempt to save her life because the bacteria had entered her bloodstream. Sadly, she died anyway. I remember that when I read about that woman, I felt so terrible about her plight, and now I needed to trust God with my life as I thanked him that my new doctor had found the bacteria and I could be treated.

It was all arranged for me to begin the treatment at the hospital the following morning. As I was leaving the house, I had grabbed my jacket and was so happy to find a rosary in the pocket, one I had misplaced and had been searching for. This particular rosary had a relic of St. Thérèse on it. I had another rosary in my purse, but this one was special. I prayed the Rosary on the way to the hospital and then held onto it because it brought me comfort.

Upon arriving, I met the nurse who would be caring for me. First, I had to sign forms noting that I was aware that the medication I would be receiving could damage my hearing and kidneys — another thing to be concerned about. I was also wondering whether I would have a reaction to the drug, since I have had severe reactions to others. As the nurse was about to start my IV, she injected me with another medication in my left arm. Two attempts to insert the IV failed; my veins weren't cooperating. I was then stabbed with a third burning injection. I clutched my rosary discreetly in my right hand and continued my prayers during the whole ordeal. "For you, Jesus. Please use this little bit of suffering for good, please sanctify it. Please let the medicine work well to kill the bacteria without a reaction, dear Lord."

Because this was happening during Lent, Jesus' passion and crucifixion were heavy on my mind. I told him, "This is nothing compared to how you suffered for me." Even though I was praying silently, the nurse looked at me and said, "At least it's not nails being driven into the palms of your hands." That was amazing for me to hear. She knew I was praying. "No offering it up here," she said in an uncanny but teasing sort of way.

"Yes, I am offering it up," I replied with a smile. The third IV worked, thankfully. It required a much longer tube up into my arm, which was very painful and remained uncomfortable day and night. It would need to stay in as long as possible, because I needed nine or ten more days of infusions. As it turned out, I would need a new IV inserted a few more times during the course of my treatment.

As we chatted, I asked the nurse if she thought I'd be able to give the retreat I was scheduled to give out of state the following week. She told me that it was very doubtful and that I should speak to the doctor. She wanted to know why I was giving a retreat, and so the fact that I was a Catholic author was revealed in my explanation. She told me that she was a Catholic but "not a very good one." I decided that I would bring her one of my books the following day. She was very happy to receive it, gave me a big hug, and wanted to buy one of each of my books. I gave her a copy of each of my books the next day.

My treatments were extended by an extra day, which meant that I would see this nurse again on the eleventh day, after her day off (I wouldn't have seen her again if I finished at ten days). On the last day, when I was getting ready to leave, this nurse hugged me tightly, right in the middle of the infusion center at the hospital, while all looked on. She continued to hug me and said, "Oh, Donna! You came into my life just when I needed it most!"

It was such a beautiful moment. I knew without a doubt that God had been working all along during our visits for my treatments and that he had used my suffering offered to him to reach this woman. Our Lord had always been in her life, but she responded to "Jesus with skin." Calcutta really is all over the world for those who have eyes to see.

MISSIONARIES OF CHARITY
54|A, A u C Bose Road.
Calcutta 700016. India

Dear Donna,

Thank you for your letter and prayers.

I am sorry to hear of the suffering you have to undergo. Jesus loves you and though He is the Lord of all – He cannot interfere with the gift of free will He has given to man. Jesus shares His love with you and shares His suffering and pain. He is a God of love and does not want His children to suffer, but when you accept your pain, suffering, death and resurrection your pain becomes redemptive for yourself and for others.

God will bless you for all the good you have done in starting the lay Missionaries of Charity in New Milford.

Be assured of my prayers. Christ calls us to be one with Him in love through unconditional surrender to His plan for us. Let us allow Jesus to use us without consulting us by taking what He gives and giving what He takes.

God love you and bless you

God bless you
lee Teresa mc

Thirteen

TAKE TIME

It takes time to do anything worthwhile. Before birth, a baby requires nine months of time and nutrition in its mother's womb after its conception. To be raised properly, a child requires time and patience from his or her parents. To blossom fully, relationships need time to grow. The list is infinite. Blessed John Paul II put it this way: "For a stalk to grow or a flower to open there must be time that cannot be forced; nine months must go by for the birth of a human child; to write a book or compose music often years must be dedicated to patient research. To find the mystery there must be patience, interior purification, silence, waiting."

In her book *Life in the Spirit*, Mother Teresa said: "Today we have no time even to look at each other, to talk to each other, to enjoy each other, and still less to be what our children expect from us, what the husband expects from the wife, what the wife expects from the husband. And so less and less we are in touch with each other. The world is lost for want of sweetness and kindness. People are starving for love because everybody is in such a great rush." I wholeheartedly agree.

We're always trying to beat the clock. Time is a precious commodity; we can't buy it, we can't control it, it can slip away, and we can't make up for it when we lose it. In most cases, time is a luxury. Yet time is something we must grab onto and also be willing to give it away to those in need. Time will rarely come to us freely — we have to seek it. It's not something we can easily part with, but we have to loosen our tight grasp on it and share it. This is where God will work. When we give him all our time, he will bless it.

I think we allow too many things to distract us and grab our attention. It's difficult not to get caught up with the endless variety of stimuli available to us today. We allow ourselves to become seduced by all the allurements that compete for our attentiveness. Granted, some of these are good things, but often we end up involved in too much, and this can cause us to miss out on what we should be doing.

Families rarely sit down to eat a meal together these days. We are too busy to make family time something important to be treasured. Gone are the days of extended families living together or near each other, regularly getting together for family meals. We are separated by distance because of transfers for work, and elderly grandparents are too often put in nursing homes. Sadly, we are too busy to care for them.

We can choose to stay at the dinner table for a few extra moments, enjoying one another's company. The Internet, homework, television, phone calls, outside activities, and anything else can wait. Family time is very precious, and it's up to us to preserve it before it disappears completely.

I think one of the primary reasons there is "Calcutta all over the world" is that we all continually feel pressed for time. We don't have time to give of ourselves; we don't have time to care for others.

We all know how quickly life speeds by, but we often wonder where the time goes. It's imperative to take the time to do what's essential. It's a good exercise to ask yourself how you really fill your time. And the question for all of us is: How can we lasso time to slow it down a bit so we can figure out what we're meant to do?

In wanting to serve the Lord as wholeheartedly as possible, Mother Teresa was driven by Matthew 25:31-46:

"When the Son of Man comes in his glory, and all the angels with him, he will sit on the throne of his glory. All the nations will be gathered before him, and he will separate people one from another as a shepherd separates the sheep from the goats, and he will put the sheep at his right hand and the goats at the left. Then the king will say to those at his right, 'Come, you that are blessed by my Father, inherit the kingdom prepared for you from the foundation of the world; for I was hungry and you gave me food, I was thirsty and you gave me something to drink, I was a stranger and you welcomed me, I was naked and you gave me clothing, I was sick and you took care of me, I was in prison and you visited me. Then the righteous will answer him, 'Lord, when was it that we saw you hungry and gave you food, or thirsty and gave you something to drink? And when was it when we saw you a stranger and welcomed you, or naked and gave you clothing? And when was it that we saw you sick or in prison and visited you?' And the king will answer them, 'Truly, I tell you, just as you

did it to one of the least of these who are members of my family, you did to me.'

"Then he will say to those at his left hand, 'You that are accursed depart from me into the eternal fire prepared for the devil and his angels; for I was hungry and you gave me no food, I was thirsty and you gave me nothing to drink. I was a stranger and you did not welcome me, naked and you did not give me clothing, sick and in prison, and you did not visit me. Then they also will answer, 'Lord, when was it that we saw you hungry or thirsty or a stranger or naked or sick or in prison, and did not take care of you?'

"Then he will answer them, 'Truly I tell you, just as you did not do it to one of the least of these, you did not do it to me.' And these will go away into eternal punishment, but the righteous into eternal life."

The fact remains: Time waits for no one. Like Blessed Teresa, we must make time to do God's will, to live out the Gospel message to serve him in each other, especially the poor and those in need. We need to take time for prayer. As Mother Teresa said, "Prayer in action is love, and love in action is service."

If a poor person dies of hunger, it is not because God has neglected him, Blessed Teresa believed — it is because "we have refused to be instruments of love in the hands of God to give the poor a piece of bread, to offer them a dress with which to ward off the cold. It happened because we did not recognize Christ, when once more he appeared under the guise of pain, identified with a man numb from the cold, dying of hunger, when he came in a lonely human being, in a lost child in search of a home."

It is incongruous that while a huge conference was being held in Bombay to discuss what could be done for the poor, a man was dying on the street from hunger practically right outside the door of the building where the conference was being held! Mother Teresa was on her way to that meeting and got lost. She came upon the starving man and brought him home to die with dignity. She was extremely sad that, while discussions were being held about what could be done in the future to help the poor, the poor were dying right there.

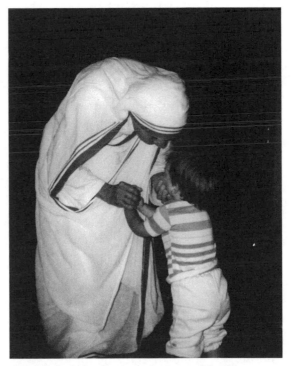

"Is this the baby that was singing at Mass?"

Mother Teresa's approach was to simply go out and feed the poor, one by one. This "one by one" spread into millions. There's no doubt that her direct manner in caring for the poor had a great impact on the whole world.

No time to love

One time the Missionaries of Charity sisters found a woman lying dead on her kitchen floor in a New York City apartment. The woman had been dead for quite some time; it was obvious that rats had been eating her body for a while. Where were her loved ones? Blessed Teresa wanted to know. She had none, the sisters found out. Where were her neighbors? When the sisters inquired, they discovered that no one even knew that the woman lived there. Were the other tenants so busy that they couldn't make time to at least say hello to each other? The fact that this woman died without anyone even knowing or caring broke Mother Teresa's heart, and it should affect us as well.

Mother Teresa observed in her book, *No Greater Love,* "It is easy to love those who live far away. It is not always easy to love those who live right next to us. It is easier to offer a dish of rice to meet the hunger of a needy person than to comfort the loneliness of the anguish of someone in our own home who does not feel loved." These are powerful words to ponder.

In Mother Teresa's opinion, the United States suffers from far worse diseases and poverty than people in Calcutta. In the United States, a lack of love and care is a serious disease. People are starving for love. We are too busy to make the effort to say "hello" to someone who lives right next door to us, much less a stranger we see walking down the street.

What I learned from Mother Teresa is that the greatest suffering is to feel alone, unwanted, or unloved. Not knowing what it really means to have a family or friends is much worse than any physical suffering. Through my correspondence with Mother Teresa over the years, I have developed an awareness of those around me that I hope I never lose.

I want to be driven by the same Gospel message that Blessed Teresa was driven by, don't you? I personally want to be told, "Come, you that are blessed by my Father, inherit the kingdom prepared for you from the foundation of the world." Don't you agree? Let's take time to pray and time to look around us to see where there is a need; let's discern where Our Lord wants us to work. We can begin by giving fully of ourselves in our own homes, and then we can reach out to our neighbor, teaching our families, friends, and co-workers to do the same by our selfless example.

Taking time

The Missionaries of Charity have a sign on the wall of their children's home in Calcutta that says:

> *Take time to think*
> *Take time to pray*
> *Take time to laugh*
>
> *It is the source of power on earth*
> *It is the music of the soul*

Take time to play
Take time to love and be loved
Take time to give

It is the secret of perpetual youth
It is God's given privilege
It is too short a day to be selfish

Take time to read
Take time to be friendly
Take time to work

It is the fountain of wisdom
It is the road to happiness
It is the price of success

Take time to do charity
It is the key to Heaven

Some questions for personal reflection

Take time to think — In your busy world, do you have time to think? Instead of allowing yourself to be overwhelmed by the demands around you, especially those contrary to your beliefs, how can you create time for yourself to think?

Take time to pray — Do you pray no matter what, no matter how you feel — even when you are tired, overwhelmed, or when your prayers feel like dry dust in your mouth? Do you set aside time to pray during the course of your day? Are you offering up your sufferings to God, asking him to bless them and make them redemptive so that they benefit others (as well as benefiting you)? Can you find moments here and there to lift your heart to God while you are involved in your work? What ways can you actively remove yourself from the busyness to become quiet and refresh your soul?

Take time to laugh — Are you so busy with your life and so serious about what you are doing that you forget to laugh? Laughter is a great medicine for our hearts and souls. Our laughter and joy of heart can be a healing balm to others, too, attracting them to the blessedness of our souls. Mother Teresa said to me on many occasions, "Keep the joy of loving Jesus ever burning in your heart and share this joy with others." How can you laugh more and then spread this joy to others?

Take time to play — St. Thomas Aquinas said: "Relaxation of the mind from work consists of playful words or deeds. Therefore it becomes a wise and virtuous person to have recourse to such things. It is necessary at times to make use of them, in order to give rest, as it were to the soul" *(Summa Theologica,* 1947). Do you make time for recreation and relaxation on a regular basis? What are some everyday opportunities you might take advantage of to slow down and be more aware of the present moment? Are there hobbies or sports that you enjoy? You're never too old to be playful!

Take time to love and be loved — What a lovely thought — to love and to be loved! What are some ways that you can increase your capacity for love? If we are stripped of everything in the world, we will nonetheless still possess love and in spite of everything, we will have love to give away . . . amazing!

Take time to give — Are you too wrapped up in yourself to give of your time, your finances, your love? How can you be more self-giving? What are some ways you can give the gift of time to meet the needs you see around you?

Take time to read — Do you feed your mind and heart with good reading materials? Do you read books together as a family? Books can enlighten your mind with useful information and wisdom to aid and inspire you on your journey and help you to guide others. Reading can also take you away from the negative influences of watching too much television or spending too much time on the computer.

Take time to be friendly — Do you say hello and smile at those you pass on the street? How about in a grocery line, or in an elevator? It doesn't cost a thing to be friendly, and it's contagious. Blessed Teresa often spoke about how a simple smile is the start of great things.

Take time to work — Do we perform our tasks with love and care? Do we strive for excellence in all we do? One time Blessed Teresa, while visiting one of her convents, came out of the bathroom smiling, visibly happy. She said: "There is a sister here who really loves Our Lord. The bathroom is sparkling clean!"

Take time to do charity — This is the heart of Blessed Teresa's message to us — to give of ourselves to love and care for others. Do you take the time to perform acts of charity in your family? your parish? your community? What are some concrete ways you can show charity in today's world?

Please, dear Lord, help me to not ever waste my time. I wish to use the gift of time wisely, whether it's at prayer, at rest, or at work. Show me the things that require my time and attention, and steer me away from the things that take me from You. Amen.

+LDM

26th October, 1991

Dear Donna - Marie

Thank you very much for your letter
and for the manuscript " <u>A Journey
of Prayer as you wait</u>"

"
Just as love begins at home, so
also peace and the woman being the
heart of the family - let us pray
that we women realize the reason
of existence is to love and be
loved and through this love become
an instrument of peace."

There is no need to include me in
the book. I pray that it does much
good.

God bless you
M Teresa mc

Fourteen

ONWARD WITH LOVE

Mother Teresa taught me to view the poor as very lovable. She always said they gave much more than we could ever give them. I have experienced this myself every single time I have served the poor and unfortunate. She reminded us that the more knowledge we have about the poor, the more we are led to serve them. They don't need our compassion or condescension — they need our love. "We are to serve [the poor] with our own hands and love them with our hearts," she said.

By serving the poor with her own hands and loving them with her heart, this humble but feisty and persistent woman established 610 foundations in 123 countries on every continent, with nearly 4,000 sisters by the time of her death at the age of eighty-seven. She also established the Missionaries of Charity brothers, fathers, co-workers, co-workers of the sick and suffering, and the lay Missionaries of Charity.

As a lay Missionary of Charity, I have led a normal life as a lay Catholic person but with a specific mission and purpose according to private vows I have taken to live a life according to the charism of Blessed Mother Teresa. The lay Missionary of Charity movement is deeply prayerful and imbued with the spirituality of Mother Teresa and the Missionaries of Charity. The specific mission of a lay Missionary of Charity is for the salvation and sanctification of our families, for the movement, and for the poorest of the poor all over the world. The vocation of a lay Missionary of Charity is simply to express to others by word and example the influence of God's love, peace, and joy in our lives. This is accomplished throughout our daily lives and in encounters with all we meet. We are mindful of Blessed Mother Teresa's words: "Love begins at home, in our movement, and in our family." We follow Mother Teresa's inspiration that "Works of love are works of peace," and that small things done with great love are very pleasing to Our Lord. Mother Teresa stressed: "Be only all for Jesus through Mary. Let us be pure and humble like Mary, and we are sure to be holy like Jesus." You can learn more about the lay Missionary of Charity movement by visiting http://laymc.com.

Graces from heaven

Blessed Teresa promised her followers that she would be able to guide each of them in a more perfect way, obtaining numerous graces for them, once she passed through the threshold of this life into heaven. As Blessed Teresa struggled for her last breath on September 5, 1997, she called out to her beloved Jesus and glanced at an image of Christ crucified that hung on the wall of her room.

Blessed Teresa's renowned reputation for holiness in her work for the poor drew vast crowds to her funeral. Her tomb continues to be a pilgrimage site and a place of prayer for people of varied creeds, backgrounds, and social classes. Her love has always transcended all barriers of religion and class, and this continues to be illustrated through the droves of multicultural visitors.

Just two days after her death, Blessed John Paul II expressed his sentiments publicly about his beloved friend. He said: "I have a vivid memory of her diminutive figure, bent over by a life spent in the service of the poorest of the poor, but always filled with inexhaustible interior energy: the energy of Christ's love. Missionary of Charity: this is what Mother Teresa was in name and in fact."

Blessed John Paul beatified Mother Teresa on October 19, 2003, just six years after her death. This is the first step to her canonization by the Church as a saint. The Holy Father referred to Mother Teresa as "one of the greatest missionaries of the twentieth century." He explained that at the heart of her mission was her deeply intimate relationship with Jesus, and her understanding of his words from the cross, "I thirst" (Jn 19:29). Blessed John Paul II said, "Satiating Jesus' thirst for love and for souls in union with Mary, the Mother of Jesus, had become the sole aim of Mother Teresa's existence and the inner force that drew her out of herself and made her 'run in haste' across the globe to labor for the salvation and the sanctification of the poorest of the poor."

Friends of Veronica

Right around this same time, Blessed John Paul gave me his blessing on my work on Blessed Teresa of Calcutta. In addition, I also started "Friends of Veronica," an outreach to senior citizens and the lonely, to imitate Veronica's loving gesture of wiping Jesus' face with her veil when he walked Calvary. I dedicated this apostolate in honor of Blessed John Paul II's twenty-five years in the papacy and Mother Teresa's beatification.

I felt God calling me to found this apostolate to serve the poorest of the poor, the lonely, the elderly, and those in nursing homes who have no visitors. I began by encouraging others to come along with me to nursing homes and hospitals to visit the people there. I arrange socials for the seniors and involve the youth of local parishes by inviting them to perform musically or visit and play games with the senior citizens. Many people have stepped forward to answer the call to volunteer at "Friends of Veronica." They feel inspired to share their time and love with those who are starving for it.

I wrote Blessed John Paul II about the inspiration I received and also about my manuscript that has become the book you are reading right now. I was amazed to receive his letter with his wonderful apostolic blessing and prayers for me, my family, my writings, and my work!

In one of Mother Teresa's letters to me she wrote, "I pray that God may bless your endeavors to start the two proposed lay associations to console Our Lord with their prayers of reparation. May you yourself be a Veronica to Jesus who is suffering in so many people — the sick, the incurables, the aged, and the unwanted — to bring them solace and strength." Her words so often brought me comfort and confirmation regarding what Our Lord was speaking to my heart and the areas in which he was directing me. I am praying that by God's grace along with Blessed Mother Teresa's and Blessed John Paul II's intercession, the Friends of Veronica apostolate will continue to flourish and serve many.

Our personal "yes" to God

Blessed Teresa taught that we are all called to be saints. This doesn't mean that we take our halos out of our top dresser drawer and polish them every morning, but rather that we open our hearts to God's will in our lives and pray to be his instruments to draw others to him. We can all answer God's call no matter what our walk of life.

Blessed Teresa said, "We are supposed to preach without preaching, not by words, but by our example, by our actions." St. Francis of Assisi said a similar thing, "You must preach the Gospel at all times, and when necessary use words." He, like Mother Teresa, shed the material things of this world and preached the Gospel by being totally immersed in it — by actually living it.

We should live our preaching too. Our actions are much more expressive than our words could ever be. We have many sets of eyes watching us at any given time. What will we choose to do for God's greater glory? Our choices ultimately influence others for better or worse.

If we're honest, many of us feel that we could absolutely become a saint if we had a different spouse, a different boss, a different roommate, a different family, or a different state of life; we could easily achieve holiness if only we had more money, less stress, less sickness or suffering, or more time. It's good to laugh at ourselves! The truth is that Our Lord, in his divine providence, puts us exactly where he knows we can best work out our salvation. We can seek holiness wherever we find ourselves — no more excuses!

Most of us are blessed with some sort of suffering; it's the reality in this life. However, Christ offers us all the graces we need to endure (and even shine) in the midst of our pain, giving us the opportunity to be an example of Christian love to others. When we give all of our pain to him, he sanctifies it and gives us peace. Let's not forget to ask the Blessed Mother for her help as well. I will never forget the prayer that Mother Teresa shared with me, which I offer to you: "Mary, Mother of Jesus, be a Mother to me now." I pray it often and hope you find comfort in it, too.

We are burnished and polished with fire at times, but never without sufficient grace to endure and to shine. Through the sanctification process, self-knowledge unfolds and becomes visible to us in our daily experiences, thus providing us with ongoing opportunities to change our attitudes and offer our lives even more fully to God.

I am absolutely awestruck by the fact that this one woman's "Yes" to God has affected millions of people around the world. Blessed Teresa's willingness to embrace poverty of spirit so completely and to blindly trust God with her life transformed her soul and opened wide her heart to the plight of the poor. Her simple message of love reached "the ends of the earth," one person at a time. She opened our eyes to see the poor all around us.

While most of us are not called to travel to Calcutta to serve the poor, we can remember what Mother Teresa said: "There is Calcutta all over the world for those who have eyes to see." Maybe our evangelizing to the ends of the earth will actually mean to the ends of our household or our workplace. We can continually expand our reach to needy souls in ever-widening circles in our local communities and beyond.

Blessed Teresa's legacy is strong and continues to live on through her sisters, brothers, priests, co-workers, lay Missionaries of Charity — and you and me. I believe that we are to carry on Blessed Teresa's work as religious and lay people, seeking Jesus in all we meet and loving him in them. I am convinced that our own personal "Yes" to Our Lord will help us to find Calcutta right in our midst, and when we follow through with our commitment to truly love our family and neighbors, we will become the salt of the earth and a light to the world. Our message of love will reach the ends of the earth and indeed change our world. Let's not forget to seek Blessed Teresa's intercession from heaven to guide us in our own ministries. She will help us find the courage, strength, and love to be a light to others.

As we answer our own individual call from God to cooperate with his work, he will shine through us so that we can light the way for others. Are we willing to allow him to shine through us, to love through us?

God calls us to go forward without hesitation, seeking holiness with hopeful and joyful hearts, being assured that our labors will not be in vain. Our work is cut out for us. We need to roll up our sleeves and dive into it with loving and humble hearts. We can live in total peace of heart when we finally surrender ourselves fully to God's will in our lives. "Accept with a smile," as Mother Teresa taught us, everything our dear Lord gives us, gratefully knowing that it's a means to our salvation.

At the end of our lives we won't be judged by how many degrees we have acquired, how much money we have earned, or how many great things we have accomplished — we will be judged by how much we have loved.

There's work to be done; let's do it.

"Keep the joy of loving Jesus ever burning in your heart and share this joy with others by your thoughtful love and humble service."

BLESSED TERESA OF CALCUTTA
(personal letter from Mother Teresa, Oct. 5, 1988)

"Teresa of Calcutta was truly a mother. A mother to the poor and a mother to children. A mother to so many girls and young people who had her as their spiritual guide and shared in her mission. The Lord brought forth from a tiny seed, a great tree, laden with fruit (cf. Mt 13:31–32). And precisely you, sons and daughters of Mother Teresa, are the most eloquent signs of this prophetic fruitfulness. Keep her charism unaltered and follow her example, and from heaven she will not fail to sustain you in your daily journey."

POPE BLESSED JOHN PAUL II
(Address on October 20, 2003, to pilgrims who came to Rome for the beatification of Mother Teresa)

Oh Lord, thank you for bringing Mother Teresa to our world that is so lacking in love. She demonstrated the joy of loving and taught us the greatness and dignity of every human being, from conception to natural death. She revealed to us how we must strive to satiate your thirst for souls and cultivate within ourselves a great hunger and thirst for you. She taught us that little things done faithfully with love are pleasing to you. Help us to turn to prayer as Mother Teresa did in order to find the strength to carry on your work.

Please, Lord, give us the strength to say "Yes" to you every morning. Bless our hearts and our hands, filling us with your grace, love, and truth so that we may preach your Gospel with caring hands and giving hearts as we go forward to serve our families, our neighbors, and our world. Enlarge our hearts, dear Lord, so that the flame you bring to our hearts will shine brightly and bring others to you, lighting the way to heaven. Jesus, I trust in you. Amen.

About the Author

Donna-Marie Cooper O'Boyle is known to millions as the friendly face and soothing voice of Catholic motherhood. Her frequent appearances on radio and television, her many books, and her speaking engagements are the public face of a life devoted to seeking holiness in the context of a happy Catholic family.

She grew up in a large, close-knit Catholic family, married, and is raising five children, the youngest now entering college. Family life has always been her first vocation, but in addition to her work as a mother, Donna-Marie has found opportunities to serve God both close to home and throughout the world. She has been a catechist for more than twenty-five years at her parish and an extraordinary minister of holy Communion to the sick, as well as a world-renowned journalist and author.

Donna-Marie's decade-long friendship with Blessed Mother Teresa of Calcutta led to a long correspondence and meetings around the world. Following in the footsteps of Blessed Teresa, Donna-Marie became a lay Missionary of Charity and founded a branch of the lay Missionaries of Charity. Today, Donna-Marie is passionate about encouraging others to follow in the footsteps of her blessed friend, caring for the poorest of the poor.

It was Mother Teresa who constantly encouraged Donna-Marie to keep writing for mothers, women, and families, and she wrote the Foreword to Donna-Marie's book *Prayerfully Expecting: A Nine Month Novena for Mothers-to-Be,* as well as back-cover endorsements for her other books. Donna-Marie was also blessed with the spiritual guidance and friendship of the late world-renowned theologian, Reverend John A. Hardon, SJ.

Remembering Jesus' request in the Gospel of Matthew that we should care for him in others, Donna-Marie founded "Friends of Veronica," an outreach to seniors, the sick, and the lonely in nursing homes and hospitals. Their goal is to bring love and comfort in imitation of St. Veronica, who lovingly gave her veil to wipe Jesus' forehead as he walked to Calvary.

Donna-Marie was invited by Cardinal Stanislaw Rylko, current president of the Pontifical Council for the Laity, to participate in an International Congress for Women at the Vatican in early 2008 to mark the twentieth anniversary of the apostolic letter *Mulieris Dignitatem,* penned by Blessed John Paul II.

Donna-Marie has been a frequent guest on EWTN television, and she discusses Catholic and family and parenting issues on a regular Ave Maria Radio segment called "Mom's Corner" at "Catholic Connection" with radio host Teresa Tomeo. She is also host of the EWTN television series *Everyday Blessings for Catholic Moms.*

In addition to her books, Donna-Marie's writing can be found in many Catholic magazines, newspapers, and on the Internet in her many columns at CatholicMom. com, Catholic Exchange, Catholic Outpost, and Catholic Online, as well as on her website and many blogs. Donna-Marie has also written a parenting column for the *Irish Family Press,* an Irish Catholic newspaper in Ireland.

Donna-Marie's work has been blessed with many awards and honors, including the Media Award from the American Cancer Society. She has received the prestigious honor of Blessed John Paul II's and Pope Benedict XVI's apostolic blessings on her books and work, along with commendations from two Connecticut bishops, Bishop Willaim Lori and Archbishop Henry J. Mansell. In addition to those honors, in 1988 she received a letter of commendation from Cardinal Eduardo Pironio, president of the Pontifical Council for the Laity, as well as several letters of commendation from the Catholic clergy and letters of acknowledgment of her work from two popes.

Keeping up with Donna-Marie

Donna-Marie travels the country to speak about prayer, motherhood, family, and women's issues. In addition, she sometimes travels internationally to speak and give retreats.

To schedule talks, retreats, and events, you can reach Donna-Marie through her main website, www.donnacooperoboyle.com, where you can also find links to her various blogs: "Embracing Motherhood," "Daily Donna-Marie: A Dose of Inspiration," "Moments of Inspiration with Your Favorite Saints," and "View from the Domestic Church." She can also be reached through email: dmcoboyle@aol.com.

Donna-Marie's Books

Catholic Prayer Book for Mothers (Our Sunday Visitor Publishing Company, 2005)

The Heart of Motherhood: Finding Holiness in the Catholic Home (The Crossroad Publishing Company, 2006)

Prayerfully Expecting: A Nine Month Novena for Mothers-to-Be (The Crossroad Publishing Company, 2007)

Catholic Saints Prayer Book (Our Sunday Visitor Publishing Company, 2008)

The Domestic Church: Room by Room A Study Guide for Mothers (Servant Books, 2011)

Grace Café: Serving Up Recipes for Faithful Mothering (Circle Press, 2008)

A Catholic Woman's Book of Prayers (Our Sunday Visitor, 2010)

Acknowledgments

To my mother, Alexandra Mary Uzwiak Cooper, in loving memory and gratitude for bringing me into this world against doctor's orders and raising me with her tender love and grace, in our large family. She taught me the necessity of prayer and how to give without ever counting the cost. In loving memory of my father, Eugene Joseph Cooper, who along with my mother brought me into this world, in gratitude for his love and support, in working hard to care for our large family.

In loving memory and gratitude to my grandmother Alexandra Theresa Karasiewicz Uzwiak, the only grandparent that I knew, for her inexhaustible love, guidance, and inspiration. Her smile, her laugh, and her lessons of love and prayer live on in my life.

Of course, a special thanks to all of my children: Justin, Chaldea, Jessica, Joseph, and Mary-Catherine, to whom every book I write is dedicated. Justin has given me consistent computer and technical help, Chaldea has offered her artistic abilities for many of my books, and all of you have been an amazing and wonderful support to me. Thank you!

To my brothers and sisters, Alice Jean, Gene, Gary, Barbara, Tim, Michael, and David: Thank you for all the great times throughout the years. Thank you for loving me.

In memory of my very dear friend and spiritual guide, Father Bill C. Smith: his amazing guidance has certainly helped to mold me into who I am. I will forever be thankful for his love.

To my godmother, Aunt Bertha Uzwiak Barosky, in gratitude for her loving prayers and guidance throughout my life, which she continues in her sweet optimistic way to bestow upon me even now.

To my husband, David, my partner and best friend: Thank you for believing in me and loving me. You are the wind beneath my wings.

In memory of Father John Hardon, SJ, my daughter Mary-Catherine's godfather and a great theologian and author who was my friend and spiritual director for many years — and actually, along with our good Lord, was responsible for my first meeting with Mother Teresa.

Special thanks to my friend Teresa Tomeo, aka Lucy, for her beautiful foreword, and my friend Dolores Teleski for her awesome photos on pages 101 and 154.

Thanks to Carmela Kube for photos on pages 24, 30, and 165.

In loving memory of Blessed Teresa of Calcutta: in gratitude for her cherished lessons of love and holy living that have deeply inspired me. Her consistent encouragement to me to continue to write in order to help others has certainly given me much courage and motivation. I thank her for her poignant and tender words and constant encouragement to me and for her quotes throughout this book. Her faith in me and love for me has left a permanent imprint on my heart.

To my dear loving Lord, to whom I owe every breath I take. Thank you, dear Lord, for your blessings and love! To his dear mother Mary, our Blessed Mother, who has always watched over me my entire life, in gratitude for her motherly influence, love, and protection that has forever been my saving grace.

In loving memory of an amazing and saintly person of our time, dear Blessed John Paul the Great: in gratitude for his inexhaustible wisdom and blessings in the profound and selfless love of his shepherding, which I was able to benefit from throughout a good part of my lifetime. I am truly honored to have his apostolic blessing on my work about Mother Teresa of Calcutta. It is so fitting that he is the one who beatified Mother Teresa, his beloved friend and sister in Christ, on October 19, 2003, Mission Sunday, before a crowd of more than 300,000 people assembled in St. Peter's Square.

With deep gratitude to Claudia Volkman and Cindy Cavnar for their wonderful encouragement to go forward with this book. A special thanks to David Pearson, senior editor of the *National Catholic Register,* for his brilliant suggestions and his encouragement to me to tell my whole story. "The world needs it," he said.

Finally, a heartfelt thanks to the wonderful team at Our Sunday Visitor Publishing Company for partnering with me to make this book possible.